Yale Studies in Political Science, 27

Saints and Samurai

THE POLITICAL CULTURE OF THE
AMERICAN AND JAPANESE ELITES

LEWIS AUSTIN

NEW HAVEN AND LONDON
YALE UNIVERSITY PRESS
1975

Copyright © 1975 by Yale University.
All rights reserved. This book may not be
reproduced, in whole or in part, in any form
(except by reviewers for the public press),
without written permission from the publishers.
Library of Congress catalog card number: 74-29712
International standard book number: 0-300-01861-4

Designed by Sally Sullivan
and set in Caledonia type.
Printed in the United States of America by
Vail-Ballou Press, Inc., Binghamton, N.Y.

Published in Great Britain, Europe, and Africa by
Yale University Press, Ltd., London.
Distributed in Latin America by Kaiman & Polon,
Inc., New York City; in India by UBS Publishers'
Distributors Pvt., Ltd., Delhi; in Japan by John
Weatherhill, Inc., Tokyo.

Contents

Prefatory Note

I am grateful to the Foreign Area Fellowship Program, the Social Science Research Council, Massachusetts Institute of Technology, and Yale University for financial support of my research.

I am deeply indebted to the following friends, colleagues, and teachers: Michiko Asada, Koya Azumi, Robert Bellah, Atsushi Fujimoto, Kyo Funaki, Tadamichi Funaoka, Kentaro Funatani, Nash Gubelmann, Everett Hagen, Tetsu Hashimoto, Fumio Imamura, Takehiko Kamo, Tadashi Kano, Ray Kathe, Noritake Kobayashi, Hideo Kumita, James Morley, Nobuyuki Nakahara, Akira Nambara, Kazuo Noda, Hugh Patrick, Lucian Pye, Naoto Sasaki, Tamisaburo Sasaki, Shozo Shikano, Toshiko Sunada, Hideo Tagaya, Kazuo Tomoyasu, and Abe Zaleznik.

My thanks for their cooperation, my admiration for their honesty and courage, and my hopes that I have not misrepresented them go to the eighty-four men who are the heroes and subjects of this book. I am grateful to them for their kindness in taking the time to answer questions that may have seemed embarrassing, disturbing, or intrusive; to complete sentences without any clue as to the appropriateness or propriety of the answer; to write imaginative stories about enigmatic pictures; to agree or disagree with statements whose meaning seemed imprecise and whose scope indefinite. If this study contributes to increased mutual understanding and a sharper perception of the universals in human value that underlie cultural particulars, it is thanks to their kindness, their intellectual curiosity, and their willingness to share knowledge and experience.

1: Culture and Politics

We are governed everywhere. But the nature of our rulers, the methods by which they are chosen, and the arguments they give to support their right to rule differ across a spectrum as broad as the variety of languages in which these things are expressed. The goal of politics is the same everywhere: the attainment of power. But the techniques of its achievement and the goals of its administration are not everywhere identical. Ultimately, we get the government we want, or are taught to want the government we get. The two ways of phrasing this are not conflicting. There is a continuous circular network of causation whereby circumstance affects belief and belief modifies behavior. Is and ought are always entwined in an embrace half antagonistic and half fruitful. Political life, a compound of concrete force and nonmaterial ideals, is the progeny. Each polity (a set of behaviors) has a political culture (a set of beliefs).

This book is about the political culture of two nations, the United States of America and Japan. They are as different from one another as may well be, and they are different, too, from most other countries of the world in the particular combination of ways of coping and arguments for justifying which defines their politics. They are interesting to study for theoretical reasons, because they are deviant cases, ideal-type extremes in the spectrum of world experience. They are essential to study for practical reasons, because they are the two most powerful nations of the economic world, because they are the most rapidly changing laboratories of human experiment in the social world, because they are extremes geographically and culturally and are as if set at odds with one another by the logic of history; because if we want to understand our future, we will find the best clues to understanding in these societies of high technology, mass consumption, human mobility and waste, and because if we want to understand our potential for variety and thereby diffuse our potential for conflict, we can do no better than to start with these two cases, so different in origin and so similar in fate.

Political Culture

In the history of political thought and experiment, the idea of political culture is one of the youngest modes of understanding. It depends on the simultaneous recognition of diversity and similarity. Most people throughout history have lived in worlds where there is only one way to live and only one set of beliefs to guide behavior. Outside the circle of compatriots there are only barbarians. This attitude can never be outgrown but only restrained and reeducated. It is the rare periods in human history that recognize not only that peoples are different and that their differences are legitimate, but also that this legitimacy rests on a basic sameness that makes diversity possible. Because our way is not the only way, therefore the outsiders are not barbarians. Because we see that cultures can differ, we see that men are brothers. It is not a coincidence that this viewpoint arises in times of revolutionary change and serves to heighten awareness of the possibility of progress. Diversity in space implies change in time. Change in time implies direction.

The theoretical principles of the study of political culture spring from insights first attained in the revolutionary eighteenth century.

It is Montesquieu who first relates the structures of government and the principles of value systematically, with his division of societies into despotisms based on fear, aristocracies based on honor, and republics based on virtue. This insight is extended to include what is now called the study of political socialization, that is to say the role of education in the shaping of men's minds and thereby the shaping of their behavior. For Montesquieu also, there is, underlying the variety of regimes and ideologies around the newly discovered world, a set of universal values. All men love liberty and hate violence. Why then are they mostly subject to despotism? Because it is easy; but moderation is difficult and rarely arrived at.[1]

Fifty years later, Herder elaborated the lasting liberal and romantic tenets of the study of political culture. The world was a laboratory or a greenhouse in which the most varied forms of human society were developed. Human nature was basically the same. It could be abused but not destroyed: "Freedom and humanity belong to the New Zealand cannibal as to Fenelon, to the gypsy as to Newton." [2] Human nature develops, bound by time and place, but all of these multiform developments have their virtues and their defects.

There is no such thing as a specially favored nation: "Least of all must we think of European culture as a universal standard of human values." [3] For Herder, God was visible in all of history, not just, as it was for his more limited and prejudiced follower, Hegel, in the parts related to ourselves.[4] Progress was possible and likely, but past

1. Charles-Louis de Secondat, Baron de la Brede et de Montesquieu, *De L'Esprit des Lois*, 2 vols. (Paris: 1961). The theoretical link between values and structures is made in chapters 3 and 4. Religious values are tied to behavior in chapter 24. Political socialization is treated in chapter 4 and the universality of certain values in chapter 5.
2. Herder is quoted in F. M. Barnard, *Herder on Social and Political Culture* (London: 1969), p. 266.
3. Herder, *Letters*, vol. 18, pp. 247–49, quoted in Barnard, *Herder*.
4. Johann Gottfried von Herder, *Reflections on the Philosophy of the History of Mankind*, abridged and with an introduction by Frank B. Manuel (Chicago: 1968), p. 213–19, and Barnard, *Herder*, pp. 184–87.

progress was valid too, and progress did not end with the present day. For Herder, as for Montesquieu, the comparative study of government and political culture led to the judgment that no government was perfect and that the more it claimed, the less it deserved: "The only government under which nature, true proportion and balance are maintained is freedom." [5]

The comparative study of values and institutions implies from its origin not the antiseptic climate of value-free analysis but a commitment to the development of political systems and political ideals which may best ensure the full development of human potential; the potential that is so multifarious and yet so mutilated in the factual data of comparative belief and behavior that they become at once the object of study and the spur to their own transformation as its result.

The study of political culture as value and idea is sometimes criticized by those who assert that values and ideas have no power to affect action but only to serve as misleading justifications for it. This powerful misstatement of a Marxian position ignores the indispensability of value positions to any scientific analysis of society. The critic who asserts that ideas do not matter must nonetheless base his own position as a scientist on several central ideas of great importance. He must believe in law, in universal regularities and historical order that can be discovered, understood and utilized. If he takes a position on social issues, he must believe that judgments of right and wrong, justice and injustice, have some objective and mutually persuasive foundation. If he believes in the possibility of improvement, and acts to bring it about, this is another way of saying that he believes in progress and the efficacy of action.

These are not obvious ways of looking at the world nor

5. Barnard, *Herder*, p. 235.

are they the only ways in which men do look at it. But the social scientist, by his action, indicates his own allegiance to them, and in so doing demonstrates and experiences that values are essential to action.

There is a continual tension in the study of political culture between the attitude that seeks to find, in comparison, reasons for the superiority of the scientist's own system, and the attitude that seeks, in the data of comparison, ammunition for the critical study of all systems including the scientist's own. But this tension is endemic to all intellectual activity—may be indeed the impetus to much intellectual activity—and does not therefore find its unique expression, but only one of its most vivid, in the comparative sciences of society. This study here presented is not free of preexistent value-based attitudes. The author is a part of one of the societies contrasted here and has political convictions that affect his vision of both. But its purpose is not to argue for the superiority of one political culture over another. In their flaws, shortcomings and built-in injustices, both societies need criticism more than praise. Their juxtaposition can help to focus criticism and stifle complacency in each.

Saints and Samurai

Political culture, compound as it is of the deepest values, beliefs, goals and self-definitions of a people, is not something about which people are indifferent. Insofar as a nation is self-consciously a nation, it creates a political culture for itself. Since the image of the self (for all citizens, the image of the nation is a part of the image of the self— this is part of the definition of citizenship) touches the deepest roots of self-esteem, it is formed with struggle, held with tenacity, defended with anger, fear, and self-delusion. If we are rarely able to see ourselves as others see us, it is because the way we see ourselves is too deeply important to us. Both Japanese and Americans, more perhaps than most other nations, have struggled to forge an identity for themselves and still struggle to defend it. The sense of uniqueness and the importance of that uniqueness is common to the heir of the Puritan "saint" [6] and the Confucian samurai.

In each case, the sense of the native tradition has become embedded in the rhetoric of politicians, the orthodoxy of the schools and the researches of scientists and historians.

In the earliest and greatest of the analysts of American belief and behavior, "laws and mores," the themes are sounded that will echo to the present. For Tocqueville, there is an inseparable link between the tenets of puritan religion and political freedom which shapes the attitudes of later generations.[7] The equality of men before God requires their equality before each other. Their struggle to achieve salvation on the spiritual level shapes their struggle to achieve success on the social plane. The loneliness of the individual before the transcendent reflects the loneliness of the liberated citizen in the absence of organic bonds of status, hierarchy, and impediments to geographical mobility.

Individualism, equality, mobility, competition: these are the hallmarks of the American tradition, the pure expres-

6. The idea that American political culture is deeply marked by its formative Puritan experience is not of course a new one. It appears in Richard Hofstadter, *The American Political Tradition* (New York: 1954) and in Carl J. Friedrich, *Transcendent Justice: The Religious Dimension of Constitutionalism* (Durham, N.C.: 1964). Another aspect of the Puritan influence is described in Francis X. Sutton, Seymour E. Harris, Carl Kaysen, and James Tobin, *The American Business Creed* (Cambridge, Mass.: 1956). Edmund Morgan, *Visible Saints: The History of a Puritan Idea* (Ithaca, N.Y.: 1963) and Michael Walzer, *The Revolution of the Saints: A Study in the Origins of Radical Politics* (New York: 1971) are outstanding analyses of the religious-political nexus within the Puritan experience.

7. Alexis de Tocqueville, *Democracy in America,* ed. J. P. Mayer, trans. George Lawrence (New York: 1969). See especially chapter 2.

sion of American values in political and personal relations. The scholarly work reflects extraordinary consensus on these basics. Hartz [8] and Devine [9] link them to the classic liberal tradition, the first with the logic of history, the second with the logic of social science. Clyde and Florence Kluckhohn [10] measure the strength of the tradition in a particularly American context of the conflict of traditions. Riesman [11] points to the loss of inner-direction with the growth of population size and egalitarianism, as Tocqueville had earlier linked equality and the exaggerated importance of public opinion. Hsu [12] and Horney [13] examine the dark side of the American political culture, demonstrating the negative consequences for the individual of unrestrained aggressive competition for success, with the consequent insecurity, tension, and fear of "failure." Potter [14] postulates that the American individualism, egalitarianism, and competitive fervor are linked to the physical abundance of the continent that offered itself to American exploitation, thus broadening and making more specific Turner's frontier hypothesis.

8. Louis Hartz, *The Liberal Tradition in America* (New York: 1955).

9. Donald J. Devine, *The Political Culture of the United States* (Boston: 1972).

10. Clyde Kluckhohn, "Have There Been Discernible Shifts in American Values over the Past Decade?" in *The American Style: Essays in Value and Performance,* ed. Elting E. Morison (New York: 1958), pp. 145–217. See also Florence R. Kluckhohn and Fred L. Strodtbeck, *Variations in Value Orientation* (Evanston, Ill.: 1961). Also pertinent is *People of Rimrock: A Study of Values in Five Cultures,* ed. Evon Z. Vogt and Ethel M. Albert (New York: 1970) which is the record of a project inspired by the Kluckhohns.

11. David Reisman, *The Lonely Crowd: A Study of the Changing American Character* (New Haven: 1950).

12. Francis L. K. Hsu, *Americans and Chinese: Reflections on Two Cultures and their People* (New York: 1972).

13. Karen Horney, *The Neurotic Personality of our Time* (New York: 1937).

14. David M. Potter, *People of Plenty: Economic Abundance and the American Character* (Chicago: 1954) and Frederick Jackson Turner, *The Frontier in American History* (New York: 1920).

For Huizinga [15] individualism and organization are the twin poles of American culture, whose fruitful struggle defines a historical development in which unity and organization seem to be consistently subordinate to variety and individualism. For Arieli,[16] the American individualism is intimately linked with the American nationalism.

For the social science orthodoxy of the 1960s, these American traits and values—equality, individualism, tolerance of diversity, acceptance of competition—are not only the purest expression of the necessary cultural underpinnings of political liberalism, but also a model to which the rest of the world can aspire as the goal of its "political development." [17] The twin errors of an ethnocentric definition of the ideal and a confusion or over-identification of ideal with reality, are not characteristic only of American thought. They are a plague endemic to all consideration of comparative values. The content of the ideal here, however, is characteristically American.

The concern for self-definition, the claim to uniqueness, and the clarity of the indigenous tradition over time are as apparent in the Japanese case as in the American. But the tradition itself is vastly different.

Where the American value system exalts equality, the Japanese tradition is said to be hierarchical. Where the American is said to be an individual, the Japanese is said to be a member of a group. Where the American practice and prescription is competition, that of traditional Japan is

15. Johan Huizinga, *America: A Dutch Historian's Vision from Afar and Near,* ed. and trans. Herbert H. Rowen (New York: 1972).
16. Yehoshua Arieli, *Individualism and Nationalism in American Ideology* (Baltimore: 1966).
17. See, for example, Gabriel Almond and Sidney Verba, *The Civic Culture* (Boston: 1963); Gabriel Almond and G. Bingham Powell, Jr., *Comparative Politics, A Developmental Approach* (Boston: 1966); and Seymour M. Lipset, *The First New Nation: The United States in Historical and Comparative Perspective* (New York: 1963).

harmony. The American puts his faith in universal law, the Japanese in particular cases; the first in reason, the second in a truth beyond reason; the American in progress, the Japanese in the past. If the American tradition is defined as liberal, the Japanese tradition is profoundly conservative.

The roots of the Japanese tradition, like those of the American, can be traced back to those ultimate levels of belief that define man's relation to the universe.[18]

Where the Puritans saw the divine as transcendent, outside the world, beyond and other, the Japanese religious tradition made no distinction between this world and that world, but saw the universe as all one: the world is just as it is and there is only this world.[19] All human hierarchies for the seventeenth-century English religious radicals dwindled to insignificance in the face of the tremendous hierarchical gulf between God and man. For the Japanese, hierarchy was broken by no such gap, invalidated by no such incongruity. The chain of awe, respect, and degree was consistent and organically graded in social, political, and religious hierarchies which were equal to and congruent with each other. Where for the early American religious dissenter all human institutions could be judged and condemned by an appeal to the transcendent authority outside and beyond them, for the Japanese samurai—bureaucrat or philosopher—the divine was in the world and the world as it was was not judged by it but sanctified. The first attitude leads to an absolute morality and a possibility of absolute moral dissent; crusades and conflicts of

18. See, for example, Robert Bellah, *Tokugawa Religion: The Values of Pre-Industrial Japan* (Glencoe, Ill.: 1957).

19. This distinction is analyzed as that between "Hebraic" and "Greco-Oriental" outlooks by Will Herberg in *Judaism and Modern Man: An Interpretation of Jewish Religion* (New York: 1959), pp. 47–56. See also Shigeru Matsumoto, *Motoori Norinaga* (Cambridge, Mass.: 1970), p. 115.

principle. The second to an absolute and unconditional reverence for this, us, the here and now, things as they are, this land, this ruler, this family and this people.

The hierarchical attitude is strengthened not only by the tradition of respect for the world as it is, but also by the concomitant idea that human nature is basically good. If men are evil, or predominantly so, they must be governed by law, tamed, restrained, and limited.[20] If they are good, law is unnecessary: justice will consist in the adjustments suited to particular cases, in compromise, in agreements related to specifics, not principles. Rulers will argue that they can be trusted and ought to be trusted; but in a political culture that postulates a radical evil in men at large, rulers can no more than others be exempt from the suspicion of wrongdoing and the net of the law.

Where the world and man are imperfect but not hopelessly so, "politics"—action, conflict, disagreement, struggle, insubordination, plots, stratagems, campaigns, mutual and overt action to control or influence power—is a good thing. In such a tradition, it is supposed with Aristotle that man is a political animal, only fully human when arguing, voting, or socially active. Where the world as it is is good, but not perfectly so, politics is bad. Conflict divides, stirs up dissent, makes power-seeking, which is shameful and disreputable, visible. In societies with the deeply conservative bent toward things as they are, harmony, not conflict, is the social virtue.

20. James Bryce characterizes the makers of the American constitution as "men who believed in original sin and were resolved to leave open for trangressors no door which they could possibly shut." *The American Commonwealth*, 2nd ed. (London: 1889), part 1, chapter 26, section 8. And Alan Simpson, in *Puritanism in Old and New England* (Chicago: 1955) emphasizes on p. 111 the Puritan belief that man is too sinful to be trusted with too much power. This idea of the origin of limited government is further explored in Hofstadter, *American Political Tradition*, p. 7: "It was too much to expect that vice could be checked by virtue; the Fathers relied instead upon checking vice with vice."

In a society of abundance, the supreme value can lie in the individual. A society of scarcity must find it in group survival. Here again conflict is a luxury. In the political world, this means that the majority must avoid pushing the minority too far, to the point, that is, where it is forced out of the consensus. Similarly, the minority is to be diffident about standing up openly in opposition. But both should ideally do their best to conceal the existence of such things as majority and minority. The watchword of this politics is "go along to get along." Another way of saying this is that the supreme political virtue is loyalty.

The hierarchy and order of the Confucian tradition, the simple optimism and nativism of Shinto, and the immobilism of Taoist thought fused by the time of the Tokugawa hegemony into a political ethic that left no room for appeal or dissent from things as they are. Motoori Norinaga,[21] the great "national studies" scholar of the eighteenth century, crystallized the political cultural imperative in a verse:

> Ima no yo wa
> ima no minori wo
> kashikomite
> keshiki okonai
> okonau na yume.

> [In this world
> you've got to obey
> this world's commandments.
> Improper behavior
> is forbidden.]

That men are good and rules are bad, that order and harmony are to be preserved at the expense of variety and conflict, that the group takes precedence over the individ-

21. Motoori Norinaga, *Tamabiko Hyakushu* in *Motoori Norinaga Zenshu,* vol. 10 (Tokyo: 1926–27).

ual, that the true source of good and standard of judgment
is here in the world, and that this nation, this people, is
unique in its commitment to these values and has its
meaning in adherence to them—this tradition of self-
analysis and self-definition extends from the political philosophers of the Japanese middle ages to the social analysts of the twentieth century in much the same way as the
American style of self-definition links puritan sage and scientific pragmatist. The difference is that the Japanese
moderns are more likely than not to deplore the tradition
even as they recognize it.

For Maruyama,[22] Japanese political culture is characterized by groupiness and social compartmentalization, by hierarchical and authoritarian systems of rule which are sus-
tained by a lack of individuation on the part of both
superior and subordinate. For Minami,[23] "vertical" structure and group "familism" combine to form a society in
which effective leadership is always subordinate to consensus and compromise. Whatever the personal value position of the analyst, there is agreement that the dominant
values of the society at large include hierarchy, harmony,
and togetherness.

If Japanese and Americans share anything besides their
respective commitment to the idea of their own
uniqueness and unique value as civilizations, it would appear from the literature to be the commitment to energy,
activism, and achievement. The goals to which this energy
is directed and the motives, personal or social, from which
it springs, may be different, but the result in both nations
has been the same: the physical transformation of the

22. Maruyama Masao, *Thought and Behavior in Modern Japanese Politics*, ed. Ivan Morris (London: 1963); *Nihon no Shiso* [Japanese thought]
(Tokyo: 1961); and Ishida Takeshi, *Nihon no Seiji Bunka: Docho to
Kyoso* [Japanese political culture: harmony and competition] (Tokyo:
1970).

23. Minami Hiroshi, *Nihonjin no Shinri* [Japanese psychology]
(Tokyo: 1953).

country and the geopolitical predominance of the state in the international sphere. Whether we regard these transformations as ominous or advantageous, there is good reason to examine as closely as possible the system of values which helps to bring them about.

The Executive Consciousness Survey

The data that form the basis of this inquiry into personal values and political culture are drawn from interviews and written protocols for which I am indebted to 84 men: 42 Japanese and 42 Americans. The Japanese filled out the 16-page Executive Consciousness Survey in 1969 while enrolled at advanced management training programs, both governmental and private. The Americans did the same in 1972 in New Haven during the course of a Yale alumni reunion.

The survey was designed to measure attitudes about personal relations in business and government. It dealt with questions of appropriate leadership techniques, modes of decision-making, and styles of problem-solving. In addition, it used direct questions and projective techniques to elicit personal feelings and attitudes about goals, fears, conflict, authority, and ultimate values. The questionnaire text is found in an appendix.

Individual goals, fears, and wishes are obviously not all there is to political culture, nor are they the most salient parts of that hypothetical entity. Political culture includes most certainly values and attitudes about specifically political symbols and institutions: flags, constitutions, parties, politicians, armies, and organizations. Beneath these specifically political aspects of cultural life, however, lies a bedrock stratum of individual attitudes to social life which supports—and defines the limits of—the political culture which flowers above it.

This survey deals not with the elaborate flowering of

specifically political values and attitudes in Japan and the
United States, but with the main trends and tendencies in
personality and values which underlie that superstructure.
It can thus make no claim to be an exhaustive description
of the Japanese and American elite political cultures, but
only of certain aspects of their foundation in the individual.

The approach employed here is firmly in the tradition of
Harold Lasswell,[24] who first hypothesized the relationship
between private motives and public objects. It is heavily
in debt to Robert Lane and Michel Crozier, whose path-
breaking studies set a pattern of excellence for the examination of how personal values relate to political views [25]
and how patterns of bureaucratic interaction may reveal
nation-specific political cultural patterns.[26] The general
principle on which research such as that of this volume is
based is that of Harry Eckstein,[27] who argued that, in a stable society, authority patterns will tend to be congruent
across the full spectrum of social groupings.

The theoretical basis of the survey and the analysis is
that of the Social Science Research Council school of comparative political culture. American-ethnocentric though it
may be in part, I have tried to avoid this pitfall as much as
possible.[28]

24. Harold Lasswell, *Psychopathology and Politics* (New York: 1960),
and idem, *Power and Personality* (New York: 1962). Chapter 10, "Politics, Personality, and Culture: The American Case," from *World Politics
and Personal Insecurity* (New York: 1965) is especially valuable on
American political culture.

25. Robert E. Lane, *Political Ideology: Why the American Common
Man Believes What He Does* (New York: 1962).

26. Michel Crozier, *The Bureaucratic Phenomenon* (Chicago: 1964).

27. Harry Eckstein, *Division and Cohesion in Democracy: A Study of
Norway* (Princeton, N.J.: 1966).

28. Gabriel Almond, *Political Development: Essays in Heuristic
Theory* (Boston: 1970); Almond and Verba, *The Civic Culture*; Lucian W.
Pye and Sidney Verba, eds., *Political Culture and Political Development*
(Princeton, N.J.: 1965); Sidney Verba, *Small Groups and Political Behav-
ior: A Study of Leadership* (Princeton, N.J.: 1961).

The men who responded to this survey were selected from a larger group to maximize the similarity of Japanese and Americans in terms of age, social status, training and career. They are all elites. They are representative of the men who are responsible for the political and economic machinery of their respective nations. Thus, their responses cannot be taken as typical of their nations as a whole, but only of that privileged social segment that is selected to make the most crucial decisions and enjoy the most extensive rewards. This is appropriate, since in all but the most extraordinary times it is the political culture of the elite that matters; that of the populace at large, insofar as it is conscious and consistent, may set the outer boundaries for choice but will not affect the act of choice itself.[29]

They work in the giant bureaucratic, economic, service, and administrative organizations which in both countries more and more monopolize resources, talent, capital, and the access to these components of social and political power.

Of the Japanese, 31 percent work in the giant ex-*zaibatsu* combines; 22 percent in the government bureaucracy; 19 percent in medium-sized firms; and 10 percent in

29. On elites and political culture see Vilfredo Mosca, *The Ruling Class: Elementi di Scienza Politica,* Arthur Livingston, ed. (New York: 1939); T. B. Bottomore, *Elites and Society* (New York: 1964); Dankwart A. Rustow, ed., *Philosophers and Kings: Studies in Leadership* (New York: 1970); Ide Yoshinori and Ishida Takeshi, "The Education and Recruitment of Governing Elites in Meiji Japan," in *Governing Elites,* ed. Rupert Wilkinson (New York: 1964); *Values and the Active Community: A Cross National Study of the Influence of Local Leadership,* The International Studies of Values in Politics (New York: 1971); Gordon J. DiRenzo, *Personality, Power and Politics: A Social Psychological Analysis of the Italian Deputy and his Parliamentary System* (Notre Dame: 1967); Robert D. Putnam, *The Beliefs of Politicians: Ideology, Conflict and Democracy in Britain and Italy* (New Haven: 1973); Robert A. Dahl, *Who Governs?* (New Haven: 1961); Samuel H. Beer, *British Politics in the Collectivist Age* (New York: 1965); Pye and Verba, *Political Culture;* Noda Kazuo, *Nihon no Juyaku* [Japan's directors] (Tokyo: 1960).

banks and insurance companies. The composition of the American group is similar, except that the last of the component groups is larger and includes a high percentage of lawyers, which is lacking in the Japanese contingent.

Within these centers of power, our respondents are power holders. Thirty-two percent of the Americans and 14 percent of the Japanese are at the top level: president, director, executive vice president; another 27 percent and 29 percent respectively are at the level immediately below the top: vice president, partner, division chief; 26 percent and 28 percent are regional manager, branch manager, production manager, finance manager, section chief, and so on. These are men who wield authority. Some of them, and not a negligible quota, wield great authority, not just within their own firm, trust, department, or organization but also within society at large.

They are born to the upper and middle classes. Forty-eight percent of the Japanese and 41 percent of the Americans are the sons of career officials, owners or top managers of business, or professionals. Twenty-one percent of the Americans and 24 percent of the Japanese are the sons of executive or "salary-man" employees of large firms. Fifteen percent of the Americans and 12 percent of the Japanese are the sons of small or medium businessmen or entrepreneurs. Sixteen percent of the Americans and 5 percent of the Japanese are the sons of the fringe professions or the honorary middle class: engineers, schoolteachers, journalists, petty officials. Seven percent of the Japanese and none of the Americans give their fathers' occupation as farmer; 8 percent of the Americans and 2 percent of the Japanese as manual worker.

They are well-educated. All of the Americans are Yale graduates. Nineteen percent of the Japanese went to Tokyo University, 24 percent to other old imperial campuses (Kyoto, Sendai, Nagoya, Hokkaido, and Fukuoka); the elite private schools of Keio, Waseda, and Hitotsubashi account for 12 percent. One out of four in each group majored in economics, 15 percent of each in science, 7 percent in business administration or commerce. Only in one respect does the training of these elites differ by discipline: 36 percent of the Japanese and only 13 percent of the Americans studied law and political science whereas 28 percent of the Americans but only 2 percent of the Japanese studied the liberal arts, literature, history, or philosophy.

In terms of birthplace, the Japanese sample is heavily skewed to Tokyo (29 percent), the Kanto area (17 percent) and the Kinki, or Osaka-Kyoto (14 percent). The American sample is predominantly oriented to New England, the middle Atlantic, and the Midwest. In both these cases the periphery and the provinces are underrepresented in terms of population.

It is fitting that they are conservative in their politics. Sixty-two percent of the Americans are Republican. Forty-eight percent of the Japanese support the Liberal Democratic Party, 24 percent the middle-of-the-road Democratic Socialists, only 12 percent the Socialists, and none the Communists or "Clean Government" Party, the Komeito.

Descent, education, position, and ideology combine to shape these 84 men in very similar ways. They are in general pragmatic, hard-working, responsible, and prudent; if they were not, they would not be where they are. They help shape in part the economic and the political destinies of their countries. They do similar jobs, they manage similar affairs, they share similar responsibilities for the success and stability of policies which are shaped to the same goals and responsive to the same interests.

But they are not the same men. They differ in their personal vision of the natural, the rational, and the desirable, and these differences are reflected in their public and private behavior. When they meet each other—and the rest of the world outside their influential but parochial cultural orbits—they find much to misunderstand, to offend, to alienate, to anger, or to enlighten.

2: Hierarchical Relations

Whatever else politics is about and whatever other spheres of value and ideology the concept political culture may cover, central to both is the human relationship of unequals. Power is at the heart of politics and is always the power of someone (or some group) over someone else (or some other group). The central dialogue in political life is between those who see the inevitable relationship of unequals as desirable, just, and legitimate, and those who see it as undesirable and unjust. The former work, in their political activity, to extend and solidify the relations of power; the latter work to restrict, ameliorate, dissolve, or abolish them. Generally speaking, it is not surprising that those who have power find themselves thinking along the lines of the first group, which is called "conservative"; and those who are subject to power think along the lines of the second group, which is "liberal," "radical," or "progressive." The interesting cases are of course those in which the powerless justify hierarchy and the powerful argue for less inequality. But it is not necessary to consider these cases here. We need only point out that in any polity there will be inequality in the distribution of power. In any political system there will also be the split between those who hold more power and those who hold less, as well as the more particularly ideological left-right split between those who defend and those who attack the principle of inequality. The difference in political cultures does not lie in the fact of inequality, although polities are certainly characterized by the degree of equality or inequality that they display, and this difference of degree is certainly not unrelated to the valuation of equality and inequality, hierarchy and collegiality, that characterizes the political culture. But more specifically, political cultures vary widely not only in how they evaluate the facts of inequality, but also in how they legitimate them. For there is inequality in every society that we know of or have ever known. And since we always tend to believe that facts, situations, and events have causes, we find reasons for them. These reasons are often taken as legitimations as well, and in the absence of arguments about reasons as causes, those who benefit from inequalities of power, materially or psychically, will seek reasons as effects. "It is right that things should be as they are because if they were not the social order would be upset . . . the gods would be displeased . . . economic production would decline . . . the crops would fail."

The legitimations of power and inequality are always related functionally to the other social values that characterize a political culture and generally they are consistent across the social structure, from the most parochial and small-scale relations of inequality (in the family, the school, the marriage) to the largest and most complex (the corporation, the army, the church, the bureaucracy, the party).[1] It is often convenient, useful, and revealing to study them not at the abstract or formal level, but at the personal. When we talk about power and its legitimation, basically we always mean some person with power over us, that power being correct and right for some reason.

Buried not very deeply in our minds are the images of the good leader and the bad leader, the king of power and glory and the tyrant with his torture chambers: good King Richard and bad King John in the time of Robin Hood and

1. Harry Eckstein, "A Theory of Stable Democracy," in *Division and Cohesion in Democracy: A Study of Norway* (Princeton, N.J.: 1966).

the Magna Carta; good President John and bad President
Richard in the turbulent American sixties. To the one we
give willing and total, ecstatic allegiance. To the other, enmity, resentment, hatred, and rebellion. Of course for different people the good may be this one or that one; the
evil also may be one or the other. It depends on the paradigm of valuation.

This paradigm is the idea of the good leader which we
share with most others in our political culture or subcul-
ture. We say that a good leader is, for example, brave,
strong, generous, wise, etc. And it follows that if a leader is
in fact brave, strong, generous, and wise, he is therefore
legitimate because he [2] fits the ideal image. And where the
leader is cowardly, weak, selfish, and foolish, then he is illegitimate because he does not fit the specifications that
our political culture has developed.

Different cultures develop different specifications for
leadership and different desired styles of leadership because the circumstances in which leadership has most
often been exercised, and therefore the techniques by
which it is exercised successfully, vary from one social environment to another. The Japanese and American political cultures illustrate this sort of variation quite clearly.
The tasks of leadership are much the same in both (the
coordination of paperwork, consultation, and innovation in
large private firms or the governmental bureaucracies that
manage, bargain with, and coexist with these private
firms). The roles and titles too, are similar: chairman, president, bureau chief, secretary, department head, etc. And
the structure of organizations does not vary within more

2. I use the masculine pronoun throughout to refer to political actors in
the Japanese and American elite environment. This usage reflects the
limited scope that women have played in both modern political cultures.
In speaking of India, Israel, Sri Lanka, or Elizabethan England, one
would not be able to make grammatical convenience and factual accuracy
coincide so simply.

than relatively narrow limits: the functional prerequisites of coordination and communication tend to make all large modern organizations whose purpose is similar resemble each other in formal structure. Nonetheless, although tasks, roles, and formal organization in the governing structures of the modern state are similar, the ideal of leadership differs from one culture to another. And insofar as this is true (and true for a reason), the style, the techniques, and the selection criteria of leaders will also vary.

The Good Leader

Table 2.1 shows in bar graph form the distribution of responses from the 84 men of the sample when they were asked to list the qualities of "the good superior." [3]

We note that the Japanese elite is much more likely to demand sincerity and warmth from its leaders, whereas the American elite demands honesty and knowledge. These highly visible and statistically significant variations in the image of the ideal leader suggest some further differences in cultural leadership style, which are pointed out in table 2.2

When we look at the ranking of preferred qualities for leadership in the Japanese and the American sample, we are struck by the high valuation of warmth and sincerity among the Japanese—qualities that, among the Americans, are either unmentioned (sincerity) or of very low rank (warmth). This suggests that the qualities specified for leadership in the two cultures are radically different in kind. That is to say, if we arrange the traits listed by our

3. Between-sample differences that exceed an arbitrary level of statistical significance of .10 (meaning that the difference in response of the two samples would arise by chance less than one time out of ten if the sampling process were to be repeated over and over) are shown beside the corresponding bars of the graph.

Table 2.1. The Good Leader

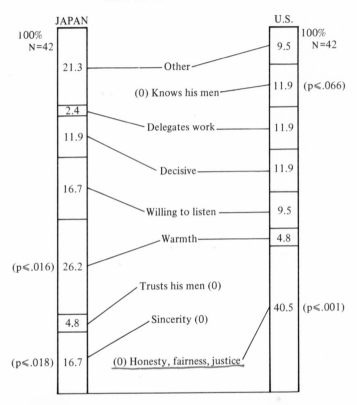

Table 2.2. The Good Leader: II

A. Traits of the Good Leader by Category

Personalistic			*Prescriptive*		
Japan		*U.S.*	*Japan*		*U.S.*
16.7	Sincerity	0.0	0.0%	Honesty	40.5%
26.2	Warmth	4.8			
4.8	Trust	0.0			
47.7%		4.8%			

	Performance		
Japan			*U.S.*
0.0	Knowledge of men		11.9
2.4	Willingness to delegate		11.9
11.9	Decisiveness		11.9
16.7	Willingness to listen		9.5
31.0%			45.2%

B. Cultural Preferences in Leadership Style

Japan: 1) Personalistic 47.7%   U.S.: 1) Performance 45.2%
      2) Performance 31.0   2) Prescriptive 40.5
      3) Prescriptive 0.0   3) Personalistic 4.8

respondents by the styles or areas of competence to which they refer, we will uncover different valuations of these areas of competence.

In the first place we may put those virtues of the leader that are concerned with his personal character. These are the qualities that define him as a person with whom a personal relationship will be pleasant or emotionally rewarding. This group includes what might be called the "nice guy" virtues. Personalistic leadership here involves the traits of sincerity, warmth, and trust.

In the second place we can define an area of competence that consists of sticking to the rules of the role. These virtues are the virtues of the man who does what he is supposed to do according to the definition of his social position. They are the virtues of correctness, of conformity to the rule book. We may call them prescriptive qualities. Honesty is a major prescriptive virtue by definition.

In the third category fall all those qualities that have to do with efficient performance of a job or task. These have in principle nothing to do with either the "nice guy" virtues or the "rule book" virtues. In this category morality is equal to effectiveness. It includes, for the Japanese and Americans of our sample, such capacities as willingness to delegate, decisiveness, knowledge of the men below, and willingness to listen or openness to information. Table 2B indicates the distribution of preferences among all these traits.[4]

It is apparent that the Japanese preference for sincerity and warmth and the American preference for honesty and knowledge are not isolated statistical artifacts. Japanese culture includes an ideal of the good leader which is primarily defined in terms of personal or personalistic virtues. The good leader is warm, sincere, and close. He trusts you. It is less important that he be effective. And his virtue as a leader, which also means his legitimacy, is, it seems, almost entirely unaffected by his propensity to conform to formal rules or fixed prescriptions. A Japanese leader does not govern or manage by the book.[5]

4. These conflicting ideals of leadership were first summarized by Max Weber in *The Sociology of Religion*, trans. Ephraim Fischoff (London: 1965), pp. 234–35: "The medieval and the Lutheran traditionalistic ethics of vocation actually rested on a general presupposition . . . which both share with the Confucian ethic: that power relationships in both the economic and political spheres have a purely personal character. In these spheres . . . a whole organized structure of personal relations of subordination exists which is dominated by caprice and grace, indignation and love, and most of all by the mutual piety of masters and subalterns, after the fashion of the family. . . . Today, however, the *homo politicus*, as well as the *homo economicus*, performs his duty best when he acts without regard to the person in question, *sine ira et studio*, without hate and grace, but sheerly in accordance with the factual, material responsibility imposed by his calling, and not as a result of any concrete personal relationship." The categories here used expand Weber's.

5. This pattern has been suggested by John Bennett and Ishino Iwao in *Paternalism in the Japanese Economy: Anthropological Studies of*

For the largest part of the Japanese contributors emotional warmth and magnanimity are the marks of the legitimate holder of authority. The ideal leader has a "big heart" (*hara ga okii*). He is "human," or rather he exemplifies in his relations with those below him a "humanness" which is an almost sensually apprehended quality. He has "the taste of a real person" (*ningenmi*). He comprehends, includes, tolerates, embraces, and accepts warmly and magnanimously. He takes care of his subordinates, "takes them under his wing" (*buka ni sewa o suru*), opens a pathway for them and guides them (*buka ni michi o hiraku*), comforts them when they are troubled (*buka no mendo o miru*). He has an almost intuitive communication with his men (*buka no koto o sassuru*) and he protects them even when they are at fault (*shita o kabau*).

What do these qualities mean in practice? Some idea of the flavor of good Japanese leadership may be gained from the comments of Tokyo bureaucrats and executives:

> The good leader has a magnanimous embracingness (*hoyoryoku*). He can be trusted. And he has to be very skillful in manipulating and softening others' feelings (*kanjo no yuwa*). Without these traits in its leader an organization cannot function, it will lack lubricating oil.

The American leader may be abrasive as long as he is fair; the Japanese may be less attentive to a mechanical "fairness" as long as he is warm and human.

One executive uses a sexual image to express the desired quality of intimacy between leader and led:

Oyabun-Kobun Patterns (Minneapolis: 1963); by Nakane Chie, "Traditional Patterns of Authority and Leadership in Japan," in *Leadership and Authority: A Symposium*, ed. Gehan Wijeyewardene (Singapore: 1968); by Noda Kazuo, "Traditionalism in Japanese Management," in *Rikkyo Daigaku Shakaigakubu Kenkyu Kiyo, Oyo Shakaigaku Kenkyu*, No. 6, special volume (Tokyo: 1963).

If you want to learn "humanity" (*ningensei*), how to deal with subordinates, you ought to spend lots of time in Yanagibashi (a geisha quarter). As Confucius said, "Women and small men are the hardest to deal with."

When you can move at ease with women and feel free in geisha society you can be at ease with anyone, and you will gain new insight into the minds of your subordinates.

What one learns from female society is the subtlety and the intensity of the emotional patterns that interweave themselves between and under the stoical and formal surface of the male bureaucracy. And one learns how to recognize, to call up and to use hidden feelings—the fear of loneliness, the desire for communion—in the service of the organization's goals, as in this story told by a Socialist civil engineer about the TAT picture of the old man and the young (see appendix B, page 190):

A young employee visits his section chief's home late in the evening to talk about a matter of business. After an intimate discussion, as the young man is getting ready to leave, the section chief looks at him wordlessly with an expression which seems to say indirectly, "I'll leave the rest up to you. . . . I ask your help and I rely on you."

A feeling of trust wells up and overflows in both of them.

These human and personal sensitivities of the good superior are summed up in a striking image from the Self Defense Forces Handbook for N.C.O.'s: "Squad leaders must act like affectionate mothers . . . [to] their squad members." [6]

Good leadership, in the American managerial culture, is

6. Self Defense Forces N.C.O. Handbook as quoted in *Asahi Evening News* (October 2, 1968), p. 8.

effective because it de-emphasizes personality in favor of the objective and efficient relationships of "the rules"; in the Japanese culture it is in large part personality that validates authority. The bureaucratic world of the big organization, rationalized and formalized though it may be, yet preserves in its authority relationships some of that primitive and ideally beautiful quality seen in the bond of parent and child or of teacher and disciple, where the only legitimacy is that which rests on love.

The Americans, on the other hand, are almost entirely unconcerned with personalistic "nice guy" virtues in their leaders. Of first importance is performance. It is as if the leader is engaged to perform a certain job and is measured and evaluated by how well he fulfills the specifications of the contract. This is of course an entirely appropriate attitude for a culture that tends to let offices to the successful bidder. Almost equally as important are the virtues of prescription, of conformity to the rules. An American leader, it appears, may be personally distasteful, cold, and uncharismatic. But he must be effective and he must maintain an appearance, at least, of honesty.

The Bad Leader

The image of "the bad leader" seems as if it ought to be the mirror image of the good leader but there is no a priori reason why this is necessarily true. The importance of the negative image in political culture, however, is probably equal to that of the positive one in terms of its effects on the techniques by which the leader is selected, those by which he governs, and the circumstances under which and techniques by which he is removed. Table 2.3 presents the Japanese and American patterns of response defining this negative image of "the bad leader."

For the Americans, a bad leader does not understand or communicate with his subordinates nor does he delegate

Table 2.3. The Bad Leader

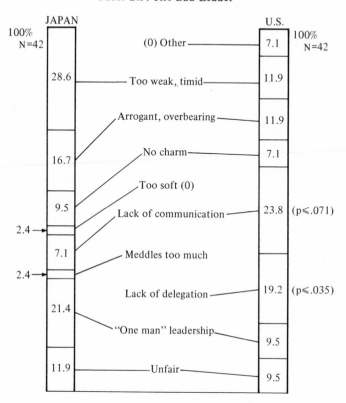

JAPAN

100%
N=42

U.S.

100%
N=42

(0) Other —————— 7.1

28.6 —— Too weak, timid —— 11.9

Arrogant, overbearing —— 11.9

16.7 No charm —— 7.1

Too soft (0)

9.5 Lack of communication —— 23.8 (p≤.071)

2.4 →

7.1 Meddles too much

2.4 →

Lack of delegation —— 19.2 (p≤.035)

21.4 "One man" leadership —— 9.5

11.9 —— Unfair —— 9.5

authority. In both of these statistically significant attitude outcroppings, he fails to perform effectively. Not quite as significant is another variation between the two cultures in which it is much more important for the Japanese than for the Americans that a leader not be weak, timid, or irresolute.

For the Japanese group, the greatest possible drawbacks in a leader are timidity, inconsistency (*chorei bokai*), irresoluteness, and vacillation (*hiyori meteki*). It may be that the Japanese leader, less desirous of authority and more concerned with preserving a warm emotional intimacy with his group, is deterred by these factors from being as authoritative as his subordinates would like. The Japanese, much more than the Americans, value emotional intimacy and use it to legitimate authority. One American contributor defines the bad leader as one who is "too familiar," a characterization that would be extremely unlikely in the Japanese context. Thus the most characteristic vices of the Japanese leader as seen by his subordinates are weakness, vacillation, and the underutilization of authority, while those of the American leader are the opposite: he is more authoritarian than he is permitted to be by the prescriptive values that define his position and his relation to those below him.

This suggests that the performance-personalism split dominates the cultural images of the bad leader as well as those of the good leader. Table 2.4 confirms this.

Personalistic traits—weakness, arrogance, and lack of charm—are the most important criteria used by the Japanese sample to evaluate their leaders. Performance traits are the most important for Americans. But while in the Japanese trait-ranking the order is the same for the bad leader and the good (personalistic, performance, prescriptive), for the Americans the order of the second and third is reversed. A possible hypothesis which could be suggested from this data is that for Americans, in the crudest

Table 2.4. The Bad Leader: II

A. Traits of the Bad Leader by Category

	Personalistic			Prescriptive		
Japan		U.S.		Japan		U.S.
28.6	Weak	11.9		11.9%	Unfair	9.5%
16.7	Arrogant	11.9				
9.5	No Charm	7.1				
2.4	Too Soft	0.0				
57.2%		30.9%				

	Performance	
Japan		U.S.
7.1	Lack of communication	23.8
2.4	Lack of delegation	19.2
21.4	"One-man" leadership	9.5
30.9%		52.5%

B. Cultural Dislikes in Leadership Style

Japan:	1) Personalistic 57.2%	U.S.:	1) Performance 57.1%
	2) Performance 30.9		2) Personalistic 30.9
	3) Prescriptive 11.9		3) Prescriptive 9.5

terms, it is more important that a good leader be honest and "fair" than that he be personally attractive. But personal traits—weakness, arrogance, and lack of charm— have more weight in defining a man as a "bad" leader than do deviations from the rules prescribed by the formal role.

The Treatment of Subordinates

One aspect of the image of the good leader and the bad leader that is particularly important is that which has to do with his relations with his followers. The tasks of authority in many cases may be oriented toward dealing with the physical world, with human enemies, or with the demands of maneuver in an abstract field: the economic market, for example, or the diplomatic arena. Yet these tasks can never be carried out without a successful relationship between superior and subordinate. Thus a crucial element of leadership of whatever kind is the content of the personal relationship of hierarchy. It is crucial in the sense that it is essential to the successful fulfillment of the governing task, and it is as much an element now as it was in the feudal system where personal relations of fealty were the glue that held the polity together. The relationship of personal hierarchy is an irreducible building block and ought to be a central object of analysis in the study of political value-systems.[7]

In an effort to approach this problem, American and Japanese respondents were asked to complete the sentence, "The best way to treat a subordinate is . . ." Table 2.5 shows the distribution of their answers. Strikingly significant statistically is the American emphasis on fairness as a criterion for the behavior of the good leader toward his subordinate. Almost equally striking is the Japanese emphasis on the necessity of the subordinate's being given interesting work to do.

The Americans also rank high the paradoxical injunction that "the best way to treat a subordinate is as an equal." This puzzling assertion is made by none of the Japanese respondents, to whom it would seem a delirious egalitarian mania. It is a contradiction in terms: superior and subordinate are *not* equal.

And yet, when one of the American respondents, senior vice-president of a giant financial institution, says that the best way to treat a subordinate is as an equal, he is not consciously indulging in hypocrisy. The cultural valuation of equality, of respect for the other as an individual, does force an adjustment in the functioning of the hierarchies of American business and government; part of that adjustment is the cooling off of personal relations, the deification

7. A good example of the kind of data and analysis we ought to have is David Halberstam's treatment of Lyndon Johnson in *The Best and the Brightest* (Greenwich, Conn.: 1973), pp. 522–57.

Table 2.5. The Best Way to Treat a Subordinate

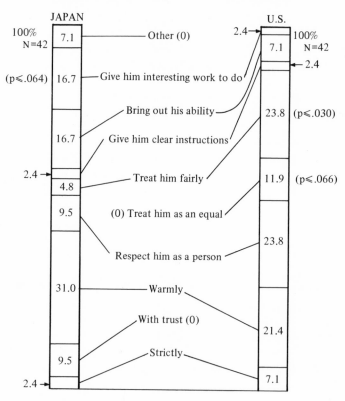

of impartiality, and the positive valuation of strictness and firmness in the enforcement of the rules. President and office boy are not equal. But when their relationship is generalized, abstracted, and depersonalized—when they are linked not by organic and personalistic bonds but by "the regulations"—then, at the very least, they can be equal "before the law."

The Americans of our sample desire just this relationship to make authority and hierarchy palatable. The Japanese desire quite another. For them, the best way to treat a subordinate is "to bring out his ability," "to give him interesting work," "to be sincere" with him, and "to trust him." Authority is legitimated, not by being depersonalized, but by personalization: not an abstract and cold equality but a particular and intimate concern. This is the mark of true leadership in the Japanese organization.

Table 2.6. The Best Way to Treat a Subordinate: II

A. The Leader's Qualities in a Good Hierarchical Relationship, by Category of Leadership Style

Personalistic			*Prescriptive*	
Japan		*U.S.*	*Japan*	*U.S.*
31.0	Warmth	21.4	0.0 Treat as an equal	11.9
9.5	Trust	0.0	4.8 Fairness	23.8
2.4	Strictness	7.1	9.5 Respect	23.8
42.9%		28.5%	14.3%	59.5%

	Performance	
Japan		*U.S.*
16.7	Give him work	2.4
16.7	Bring out his ability	7.1
2.4	Clarity of instructions	2.4
36.8%		11.9%

B. Cultural Preferences in the Good Hierarchical Relationship

Japan: 1) Personalistic 42.9%   U.S.: 1) Prescriptive 59.5%
       2) Performance 36.8   2) Personalistic 28.5
       3) Prescriptive 14.3   3) Performance 11.9

This helps us to begin to answer the question, "What do we want of our superiors?" It is a question the answer to which those in authority in any culture would do well to know.

The Japanese want a relationship on the personal level. They are concerned with the qualities of interpersonal emotion—warmth, trust, and strictness. They place relatively little importance on the rules that might be made to govern the relationships of hierarchy. In Japanese political culture, the relation of superior and subordinate is ideally no more formal and no less intimate than the relationship of friends, lovers, or members of a family.

The Americans, on the other hand, while concerned with personal qualities to a certain extent, place primary emphasis on the proper observation of the imperatives or rules governing hierarchy. Fairness and respect for the individual have nothing to do with a personal relationship. In fact, since they are based on the idea of ignoring the personal ("the law is no respecter of persons"), they are the antithesis of the Japanese insistence on the emotional quality of the interpersonal tie. The American response is also colored by a strongly felt cultural bias away from hierarchy itself, which we will have occasion to discuss later. This is reflected of course in the implication ("the best way to treat a subordinate is as an equal") that the best hierarchical relationships are not hierarchical at all.

The qualities characterizing a "bad" hierarchical relationship for the two cultures are detailed in tables 2.7 and 2.8. The ranking of traits disvalued in the relationship of hierarchy is congruent in large part with that of those valued. But here, for the Americans, prescriptive qualities lose their usual preeminence and personalistic qualities rank first in importance.

The explanation seems to be in the extreme importance for the American group of the trait cluster of cruelty, arrogance, overbearingness, and harshness in characterizing

Table 2.7. The Worst Way to Treat a Subordinate

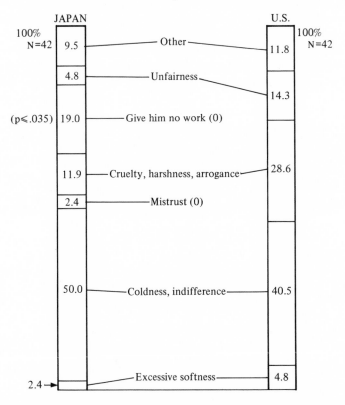

the attitudes of the bad leader. This must be labeled a personalistic criterion since it is a function of individual behavior rather than a formal violation of the prescriptions
governing leadership roles. There is nothing in the rule
book that says a superior cannot be harsh, cruel, sadistic,
arrogant, or overbearing to his men. Or is there? Perhaps
the antihierarchical bias of American political culture has

Table 2.8. The Worst Way to Treat a Subordinate: II

A. The Leader's Qualities in a Bad Hierarchical Relationship, by
   Category of Leadership Style

	Personalistic			*Prescriptive*	
Japan		*U.S.*	*Japan*		*U.S.*
2.4	Mistrust	0.0	4.8%	Unfairness	14.3%
50.0	Coldness	40.5			
2.4	Being too soft	4.8			
11.9	Cruelty	28.6			
66.7%		73.9%			

	Performance	
Japan		*U.S.*
19.0%	No work	0.0%

B. Cultural Dislikes in the Bad Hierarchical Relationship

Japan: 1) Personalistic 66.7%   U.S.: 1) Personalistic 73.9%
       2) Performance   19.0   2) Prescriptive   14.3
       3) Prescriptive   4.8   3) Performance   0.0

reached the point where personal attitude and behavior
are legislated and prescribed for hierarchical relationships.
If it is true that enlisted men can accuse officers, and work-
ers can challenge foremen *through the judicial process* for
acts of arrogance or harshness, then we can classify this
category of valuation as one of prescription rather than
personality (as, for example, one could not in the Prussian
Army or the British Navy of two hundred years ago). Then
the balance of the American sample's preferences and dislikes would be more congruent with the other evidence.

There are some data to suggest that this is indeed the explanation.[8]

The American rejection of the bad superior is personalist in that his fault, cruelty or harshness, is a personal quality. It is prescriptive inasmuch as the same harshness is seen to violate the norms of behavior culturally sanctioned in the American political culture of hierarchies. It is impossible, with the data at hand, to settle the question of predominance more precisely. It is useful to point out, however, regardless of the weight of prescriptive and personalist elements in the image of the bad leader, that the personalist qualities most strongly condemned are different for Japanese and Americans. A bad leader for the Japanese is a cold one—impersonality in itself is a sin. For the Americans the worst sin is not impersonality but the infringement on the rights of individual personality implied in cruelty or harshness.

Both Japanese and Americans agree in general that one of the worst ways to treat a subordinate is to ignore him—to be cold, indifferent, and to treat him as a tool. The man below you is still a man. But they diverge in their estimate of what constitutes the worst affront to that humanity.

If equality and intimacy, respectively, are the qualities that the subordinate seeks in his relationship with his superior, the situations he fears are those of inequality and exclusion. The second largest single category of American responses is that which points to arrogance, authoritarianism, browbeating, or a cruel autocracy as the worst flaw in the superior's use of authority. Almost 30 percent

8. U.S. Judge Advocate General's Office, *Index and Legislative History, Uniform Code of Military Justice*, House of Representatives, 81st Congress, 1st session, 1950, report #491, p. 101, article 93: "Any person subject to this code who is guilty of cruelty toward or oppression or maltreatment of any person subject to his orders shall be punished as a court-martial may direct." But of course the content of "oppression" depends on the cases and precedents.

of the Americans, but less than half that proportion of the Japanese, fall into this set. Ten percent of this American group specifies that the worst way to treat a subordinate is as an inferior; it occurs to none of the Japanese to make the distinction, strained perhaps but essential for their western counterparts, between being of lower rank and being less good. Indeed, this distinction is not a natural one and it would seem incomprehensible, perverse, or useless in more simplistic political cultures, in which "of higher rank" of course means "better."

If the Americans in our sample show a deep sense of the illegitimacy of inequality, the Japanese have an equally deep sense of the illegitimacy of exclusion. The worst way a superior can treat those below him, in their view, is to *leave them out* of things: to give them no work to do, to distrust them. In Japanese political culture, ideally, everyone is hierarchically unequal but everyone belongs. In the American, everyone is alone, but everyone is equal.

To offend his men as deeply as possible, a Japanese manager has only to leave them out, as in this description of the first Thematic Apperception Test picture: [9]

> Three executives in an office, discussing something they want to keep secret from their subordinates.
>
> It had to do with work rules. I was about to enter the room. They didn't notice me. I tried to listen and to hear what the man at the desk in front was saying, then I thought, "I can't go in now, it would be bad manners. I'll come back later."
>
> The executive facing me must have known I was there, but he pretended not to notice. It would have been much better if he had acknowledged me, even if only a little. I felt deeply the secret coldness of these men.

9. For the picture, see p. 189 in appendix B. Like all the TATs, this is patterned after Solomon's modifications.

An American manager, on the other hand, to offend his men as deeply as possible, treats them as inferiors. The Japanese subordinate does not mind being pushed around so much if he is pushed around personally. The American does not mind being treated coldly as long as he is treated fairly. One can imagine the latter, referring to his boss: "Well, he's a tough old bastard, but he's fair." The former would say, "He may be unfair and arbitrary, but he's warm."

The images of what a leader ought to be and the relative importance of the criteria by which he is judged are thus quite different in Japan and America. The consistency of these images also differs.

For the Japanese, the ranking of personality, performance, and prescriptive traits of style is consistent across all measurements. A good leader is predominantly warm and sincere: personalist. A bad one is weak, makes one-man decisions, and is arrogant and overbearing: personalist. Treating one's subordinates well means giving them personal warmth and work. Treating them badly means giving them no warmth and no work. A good leader is above all a good person, one who can be loved and respected regardless of his performance in the objective demands of his task. Least of all is he judged by conformity to a set of rules outlining the duties and responsibilities of his role. Honesty, not cutting corners, doing things according to Hoyle, are not qualities that seem to our Japanese sample to be importantly relevant in judging the quality of leadership.

For the Americans, the image of the good leader is not consistent but varies according to whether the question is considered in the abstract or with regard to the specifically personal relationship of superior and inferior. The good leader in the abstract is judged primarily by performance, secondarily by prescription, and lastly by personality. That he get the job done is of first importance, that he do this correctly and by the book is of secondary importance, and what he is like as a person is of only minor weight. But when the Americans think of the relationship between superior and subordinate, performance slides to last place. Now, as with the Japanese, personality assumes greater importance; but prescriptive values—fairness—maintain their centrality.

In the Japanese context, a leader is defined by how he manages his personal relations; in the American context, by how he manages his job. For Americans, in addition, the aspect of conformity to the rules—those governing both the job and the people associated with it—is of relatively great importance; for the Japanese, it is relatively minor.

The Good Follower

The Japanese emphasis on personality and the American emphasis on prescription and performance are visible also in their descriptions of the traits of the good and the bad subordinate. For the Japanese, a good subordinate is a source of original and valuable ideas. He thinks, he makes a contribution. His principal virtue is thus a performance virtue—see tables 2.9 and 2.10. Secondarily, he is harmonious, friendly, and understands his superior. These are the versions of the Japanese personalist virtues suited to the lower ranks.

For the Americans, a good follower is one who knows his place and who acts according to the rules governing it. Thus he has primarily only to act respectfully and loyally. His personal qualities are only incidental. It is important secondarily that he perform well, in the sense that he acts by himself, takes initiative, and is a "self-starter." But performing well is secondary to performing according to the rules.

In his subordinates, the American wants loyalty, depen-

Table 2.9. The Good Subordinate

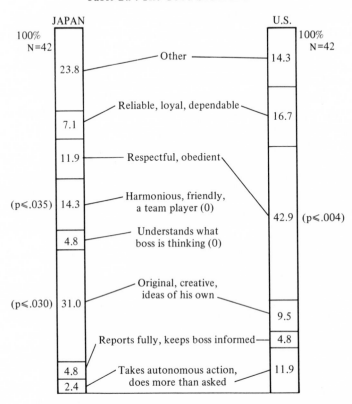

dability, character, reliability, respect, and obedience. The
Japanese, for his part, wants friendliness, humanity, a harmonious nature, the quality of good "team membership."
For this group, the good subordinate is also one who understands and trusts the superior.

The demand for the abstracted and depersonalized relationship, then, is not one made only on American superior
by American subordinate. The boss demands of the one
below him too only that he should act according to the
rules, be reliable and respectful. Reliability and respect
are the "fairness" of the one below to the one above. Dis-
respect and disobedience, for Americans, are a breach of
the minimum terms of the superior-subordinate contract.

The demand for intimacy, understanding, and inclusion
is not made only by the Japanese subordinate. His boss too
asks that he be understood, that he be trusted, and that he

Table 2.10. The Good Subordinate: II

A. Qualities of the Good Subordinate by Category

	Personalistic			*Prescriptive*	
Japan		*U.S.*	*Japan*		*U.S.*
14.3	Harmonious	0.0	11.9	Respectful	42.9
4.8	Understands	0.0	7.1	Loyal	16.7
19.1%		0.0%	19.0%		59.6%

	Performance	
Japan		*U.S.*
4.8	Reports	4.8
2.4	Active	11.9
31.0	Ideas	9.5
38.2%		26.2%

B. Cultural Preferences in the Good Subordinate

Japan: 1) Performance   38.2%   U.S.: 1) Prescriptive   59.6%
        2) Personalistic 19.1   2) Performance   26.2
        3) Prescriptive 19.0   3) Personalistic 0.0

be included. Not only the subordinate, but the superior too, can be deeply wounded by exclusion:

> The title of the picture is "The Section Chief Ignored."
>
> A conference has just finished and three employees are still debating some problem.
>
> The section chief has already officially closed the meeting, so he can't enter the room frankly and openly. He is anxious; now he wishes he hadn't left his seat in the conference room.
>
> Afterwards he asks his secretary, who was taking notes, what they were all talking about. The secretary gives him a vague and ambiguous answer.
>
> The coolness between the section chief and his men increases.

Here, paradoxically but not surprisingly, the qualities of the good subordinate are not the opposite of those of his chief but their mirror image. Both master and man in the Japanese context want human warmth, friendly understanding, and intimacy from the other. Both master and man in the American context want the mechanical relationship of playing by the rules: let the boss be fair, let the subordinate work hard. This fulfills their mutual obligation.

The mechanical quality of the American authority relationship simulates the relationship of equals; the intimate quality of the Japanese relationship makes a relationship of unequals acceptable.

The Bad Follower

A bad subordinate for the Japanese (see table 2.11) is one who is tricky, deceitful, and untrustworthy—personalist criteria—and one who fails to make his proper

Table 2.11. The Bad Subordinate

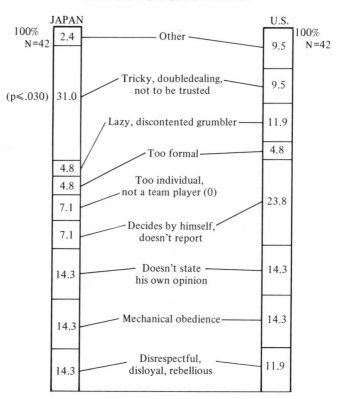

contribution to the task at hand. He is only mechanically obedient. For the Americans, a bad subordinate fails primarily in performance: he does not report, he acts on his own, exceeding his authority (this is the vice that belongs to the virtue of "being a self-starter"). Again, he fails personally—he grumbles, is lazy, malingers. The bad subordinate, for both Americans and Japanese, is the one who disappoints the conditioned expectations of his culture.

For the Japanese, who expect and hope for trust, sincerity, and intimate understanding, the worst discovery one can make of a subordinate is that he cannot be trusted and that his protestations of friendship and loyalty have been *insincere*. The largest single category of Japanese responses here is composed of epithets like "doubledealing," "toadying," "not to be trusted," *"makes a fool of the boss."* The Japanese also criticize the bad surbordinate as

Table 2.12. The Bad Subordinate: II

A. Qualities of the Bad Subordinate by Category

	Personalistic			*Prescriptive*	
Japan		*U.S.*	*Japan*		*U.S.*
4.8	Too formal	4.8	14.3%	Disrespectful	11.9%
31.0	Tricky	9.5			
4.8	Grumbles	11.9			
7.1	Loner	0.0			
47.7%		26.2%			

	Performance	
Japan		*U.S.*
7.1	Doesn't report	23.8
14.3	Doesn't state own opinion	14.3
14.3	Mechanically obedient	14.3
35.7%		52.4%

B. Cultural Dislikes in the Bad Subordinate

Japan: 1) Personalistic 47.7%   U.S.: 1) Performance 52.4%
2) Performance 35.7   2) Personalistic 26.2
3) Prescriptive 14.3   3) Prescriptive 11.9

"too individualistic," "not a team player," and so on. This view finds no echo among the Americans in this sample.

For the latter, the principal complaint about those below them is one that grows out of the American pattern of de-personalization. The bad subordinate is one who does not report or consult. He makes the authority relationship so abstract that even the communication necessary for ef-ficiency begins to fade away. The Japanese manager has not so much occasion to complain of this fault. His men are only too eager to be included, to share, to confer.

For the Japanese leader, the sins and the virtues of his followers are personal—sincerity or treachery, excessive individuality, or true "membership." For his American counterpart, virtue and vice in subordinates consist in the degree of approximation to the rules, to the canons of ef-ficiency, equality, and impersonality by which a good hier-archical relationship is measured.

If these data are taken together as a whole, and we con-sider only the relative importance of the traits of style by which judgments of good and bad seem to be made, we might arbitrarily assign 3 points to a ranking of first impor-tance, 2 points to one of second importance, and 1 point to a ranking of third. Then the total rankings would be, for the Japanese: personality 17, performance 13, pre-scription 6; for the Americans: performance 13, prescrip-tion 12, and personality 11. The use of numerals here implies only the ordinal degrees of greater and lesser, but it can serve to impress us concretely with the vast spread of subjective weight between personalistic criteria and prescriptive, in the Japanese case, and in the Ameri-can case with a relatively balanced array of criteria in which performance nonetheless is emphasized and per-sonality is played down.

Another way to analyze the data as a whole is to con-sider not the criteria used for judgment but the specific traits singled out by each sample in its collective image of the good and the bad relationship of hierarchy. We can distinguish four paradigmatic images of the relationship of superior and subordinate in this way: the Japanese ideal, the American ideal, the Japanese anti-ideal and the American anti-ideal. These collective images may be taken to represent the hopes and fears, the positive and negative poles, the extreme map coordinates within which and guided by which the drama of leadership, authority, and submission plays itself out in the two cultures.

In the Japanese ideal, the leader is warm, charming, sincere. He trusts his subordinates, treats them warmly, and gives them interesting work to do. They reciprocate with original ideas, valuable contributions of energy, effort, thought, and harmonious teamplayer behavior.

The Japanese anti-ideal is one in which the leader is not warm but cold, not human but ignores his subordinates, does not give them interesting work but leaves them out of the decision-making process. He is a one-man leader, he is arrogant, or he may be timid, weak, and vacillating. His subordinates reciprocate with deceit, a facade of good behavior (*goma-suri,* toadying, ass-kissing), and mechanical obedience in place of active contribution.

The important factors in the Japanese estimate of the quality of leadership and the hierarchical relationship are personal warmth, trust, sincerity, and the sharing of work and initiative. The task is a team effort. Hierarchy does not mean a fragmentation of the organizational group.

The American ideal is the leader who performs well. He delegates responsibility, acts decisively, and knows his men. He is fair, honest, and plays by the rules. His relationship to his subordinates is characterized by his respect for the rules which govern that relationship (by fairness), and his subordinates reciprocate by following the rules of their own roles. They are respectful, loyal, obedient, and actively helpful.

The anti-ideal is one in which performance fails—the

leader does not communicate or delegate. He treats his
subordinates harshly, arrogantly, indifferently, and un-
fairly, thereby making illegitimate the kind of authority
that is supposed to be exercised only according to the
rules. Those below reciprocate by laziness, grumbling,
and failure to report or to keep him informed.

The important factors in the American vision of the pos-
sibilities of the hierarchical relationship, for good and bad,
are performance, sticking to the rules, and mutual respect
for what the rules of relationships demand from the other:
from the superior, fairness; from the subordinate, respectful obedience. The task is fragmented by delegation, not
shared. Jobs are specific and individual. Relationships are
shaped by conformity to the rules that govern them, not by
the interaction of persons as personalities.

Authority in Japan is personal, shared, unstructured, and
judged by sincerity and trust. In America, authority is allo-
cated and structured by prescriptive rules and judged by
performance.

Authority in Action: Two Cases

How these ideal and anti-ideal relationships of superior
and subordinate may work out in practice is suggested by
data from two questions in the survey. These are the cases
of "the letter of recommendation" and "the decline in production." [10]

1. The Letter of Recommendation
    One of your subordinates wants to leave his job and
asks for a letter of recommendation. You don't want to
write such a letter, but the subordinate keeps asking for
it. In this sort of situation which of the following courses
of action would you choose?

10. These were devised by Hanfmann and Getzels. See note 23,
chapter 1.

a. Refuse flatly.

b. Agree to write the letter, but give in it a true and unfavorable opinion of the subordinate's character.

c. Give his formal job record only.

d. Give in to his urging and write a standard letter of recommendation.

e. Other.

This question serves to make explicit some of the consequences in action of the relationship of hierarchy in the Japanese and American political culture. The responses are shown in table 2.13. Most of our contributors from both groups see the situation described as unproblematic. In proportions that vary only slightly, they are likely to refuse or to send a work record only. The remaining one third, however, develops more complex strategies and their emphases, their rationales, and the values that lie behind them differ.

Fourteen percent of the Japanese, but none of the Americans, write that they will give in to the urging of the subordinate. We see here that one of the consequences of the personalistic relationship between master and man in Japanese political culture may be a greater degree of malleability on the part of the superior. Although they are more hierarchical and less a relationship of "equals," the Japanese bonds of authority allow the man below more freedom in certain cases and the man above less, because they are tied to each other, or are supposed to be, not by rules but by personal relationships.[11]

11. This is sometimes suggested in the literature. That the leader in Japanese political culture is pliant and dependent on his subordinates has been argued by Nakane, "Traditional Patterns," and L. Takeo Doi, "Amae: A Key Concept for Understanding Japanese Personality Structure," in *Japanese Culture: Its Development and Characteristics*, ed. Richard K. Beardsley and R. J. Smith (Chicago: 1962), and L. Takeo Doi, "Some Aspects of Japanese Psychiatry," *American Journal of Psychiatry*, vol. 2 (1955), p. 691. A similar view is expressed by Maruyama Masao in "Thought and Behavior Patterns of Japan's Wartime Leaders," in

Table 2.13. The Letter of Recommendation

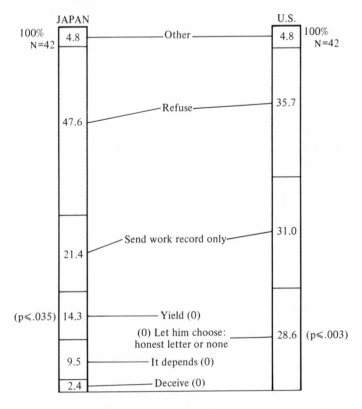

One of the Japanese, none of the Americans, writes that he would deceive the subordinate by appearing to yield to his request but actually giving him a letter of nonrecommendation. Social pressure forces this deceit, because the boss must find a solution that avoids open disharmony and conflict and yet allows him his prerogative of leadership and decision. If the collision between the social demands of intimacy and harmony and the functional demands of action is too destructive, the leader may seek to slip out from between the two opposing forces in some such way as this. Of course the likelihood of such compromise-deception solutions in cases of irreconcilable conflict gives rise to endemic suspicions of insincerity, disloyalty, treachery, and so on. But this is the way in which social values at times create social situations that force their own abandonment; and abandonment leads to a more fervent affirmation of the ideal. Thus our values must be emphasized more strongly the less able we are to live up to them.

Nine and one half percent of the Japanese and none of the Americans suggest "other" solutions of the type: "it depends on why he wants the letter" or "it depends on how long he has been with the firm" or "it depends on how well you know him" or "on where he is going." It depends!

The deepest wisdom of human relations for Japanese culture, where no two cases are the same and where no general rule can take care of all contingencies, is the formula that applies if, as here, there is obviously not enough information to make any judgment.

But the Americans feel no such cautious sensitivity to the depths of the social situation and no such reluctance to make a decision on less than adequate information. Twenty-eight percent of them suggest an "other" strategy

---

Thought and Behavior in Modern Japanese Politics, ed. Ivan Morris (London: 1963).

that occurs to none of the Japanese contributors. This is the strategy of openness, noncoercion, and playing by the rules. To wit, "Talk to the subordinate frankly and lay your cards on the table. Bring the situation out in the open. Let him choose whether he wants a true letter or no letter at all." This solution appeals to all the qualities prized in the American managerial political culture—openness, equality, free choice. How high-minded and "fair" this boss is! He does not make the decision, he leaves it to his subordinate. He does not evade the problem, he faces up to it. He is not arrogant or authoritarian, he appeals to the subordinate for *his* decision.

But appealing to openness and free choice presents the subordinate with a pair of losing alternatives. He does not really have a choice between a bad letter and no letter at all. Who needs a letter of nonrecommendation? Playing the game by the rules, out in the open, and respecting the subordinate's "equality" may seem hypocritical, sadistic, unfeeling, and irresponsible to the more sensitive Japanese executive. He thinks, at least, when he says "it depends," that there may be a dying wife and ten children. When he chooses to write a true but unfavorable letter, unbeknownst to his subordinate, he spares him at least the unbearable shame of knowing that he is thought to be no good.

The preference rankings (in percentages) in the Japanese and American samples for the three solutions to this managerial problem are similar:

Japan: 1) Refuse   47.6   U.S.: 1) Refuse   64.3
       2) Compromise 33.3   2) Compromise 31.0
       3) Yield   14.3   3) Yield   0.0

What we note in particular is the greater weight of solutions by the book—prescriptive solutions—in the American case. Almost 60 percent of the American sample seek instinctively for a judgment that will be impersonal and authoritative because of its generality: 28.6 percent "let him choose," 31.0 percent "work record only." Only 21.4 percent of the Japanese prefer such solutions.

The Japanese weight of choice is in another direction. Outright refusal is the performance-oriented solution. It solves the problem brutally and effectively with little waste of time or effort. But, following this choice, in second place, 26.2 percent of the Japanese and none of the Americans choose personalist strategies: 9.5 percent "it depends," 14.3 percent "yield," and 2.4 percent "deceit."

So the style of authority in this hypothetical case study varies just as did the ideal and anti-ideal of leadership in the earlier data:

Japan:			U.S.:		
1) Performance	47.6		1) Prescriptive	59.6
2) Personalistic	26.2		2) Performance	35.7
3) Prescriptive	21.4		3) Personalistic	0.0

2. The Decline in Production

The chief feels that the men under him are not doing a very satisfactory job. He asks his superior what he should do and the superior tells him not to worry, that things will take care of themselves. But still day after day the output of the group goes down while other departments seem to work at full capacity.

In this kind of situation, which of the following courses of action would you pick?

a. Have a friendly and intimate discussion with your subordinates and try to find out what the cause of the problem is.

b. Intensify discipline and crack down on your subordinates.

c. Work through one of your trusted subordinates to find the source of the problem.

d. Confer with your superior and try to get him to take the responsibility for corrective action.

e. Other.

Table 2.14. The Decline in Production

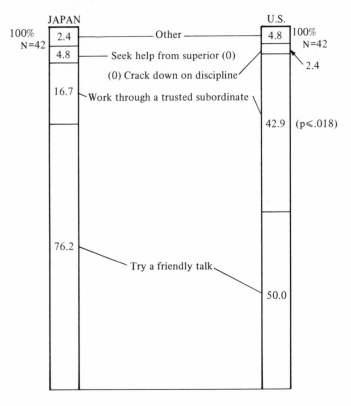

Both Japanese and Americans in this case show themselves very little inclined to resort to harsh disciplinary
measures, which seem in general to be seen by both as
more appropriate at the lower levels of any hierarchy than
at the top (see table 2.14). They are equally disinclined to
try to pass the responsibility on up to a superior level. This
strategy too, may be appropriate or productive at lower
levels, but at the elite level of these respondents it is probably felt that it would be regarded as a confession of in-
competence.

The favored solution of both groups is the "friendly
talk" tactic. This strategy jibes particularly well with the
Japanese preference for intimacy, personal contact and
group discussion in problem-solving. But the Americans
are much more likely than the Japanese to adopt the "work
through a subordinate" strategy. The reason may be con-
jectured to lie in the way this strategy is perceived by each
group.

For the Americans, it is seen as performance-oriented
and virtuous. Delegation of authority and responsibility is
one of the things that a good leader does. For the Japanese, it is a personalistic mistake. Working through a
trusted subordinate is not to open but to conceal oneself
and one's intentions behind a facade. It is relegating a
group problem away from the group to a special clique of
trusted favorites whose status implies mistrust of those
outside. It smacks of cliquishness, factionalism, and facade—the vices and malfunctions to which the Japanese
authority relationship is particularly prone and of which
the decision-making elite is particularly wary.

Japanese and American political cultures are distinguished by the different personal traits they value in the
holders of authority, by the differing prescriptive rules
they make for the incumbents of hierarchical roles, and by
the ways in which they measure performance. But at a
more abstract level they are distinguished not only by the

different contents of these categories but also by the different weights these categories are given in the judgment of good and bad. It is important that the personal traits disliked or disvalued in a leader are weakness and timidity for the Japanese and arrogance for the Americans. This tells us something about what the people of each culture want and what they get in personal terms. It is even more important to know that while personal traits are highly important for the Japanese in evaluating the legitimacy or goodness of their leadership, they are much less so for the Americans, for whom performance and prescriptive traits are more important. This tells us not only what the people of each culture want, but also how they judge what they get, in terms that go beyond the personal.

3: Authority and Power

The last chapter explored one basic aspect of the political culture of elite Japanese and Americans, in their attitudes toward the person of the leader. This exploration reveals that for the Japanese, power becomes legitimate primarily because of personality; for the Americans, power is accepted as rightful because of performance and prescription. This cultural difference in what is expected from managers, administrators, or rulers, and in how they are evaluated, implies further differences of attitude toward authority and power in general. This chapter deals with these latter.

Most basic is a wide variance in expectations as to how power is regarded as likely to be used. Table 3.1 shows the two groups' aggregate completions of the unfinished sentence: "In a position of power, he . . ."

The modal answer for the Americans is one indicating an expectation that power is ordinarily used well, responsibly, or with concern for the rights of those subject to it. None of the Japanese sample gives such a response. The modal answer for the latter is one that suggests that the principal concern of those in power is to hang on to it. None of the Americans gives such a response. Japanese are also more likely to consider that those in power will be corrupt, lazy, degenerate, blind, foolish, or overconfident. They expect, more than Americans, that power-holders will be authoritarian, harsh, arrogant, or cruel. Americans are more likely to suggest that power-holders are uncertain or unsure of themselves.

Table 3.1. In a Position of Power

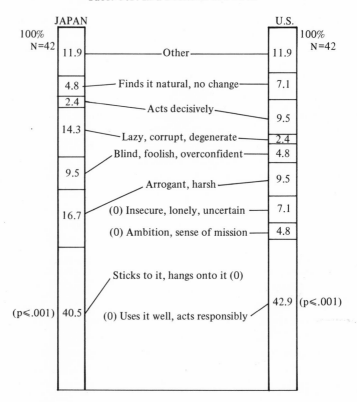

Cultural values are the offspring of historical experience, and it is perhaps to history that we should turn for an explanation. Most simply of all, we can say that the iconic image of American political values is the revolution against power misused and that from the foundation of the United States there has been an explicit concern for the limitation of power. The history of Japan, on the other hand, is one of anarchic struggle and civil war or authoritarian domination, with nothing between these two extremes, for almost two millenia. How should the Japanese not welcome authority? And yet they cannot but expect to see it misused. Is it possible that Japan must kill a king as in 1649 and defy another in arms as in 1776 before power can be demystified and treated (perhaps overoptimistically) as only a tool to be used rationally for the common good? The American, with his alleged tastes for change, conflict, and equality, and the wounds of regicide and rebellion long since scarred over, might give a casual assent. For most Japanese the medicine would seem too strong for the complaint.

This finding is corroborated by the stories told about the Thematic Apperception Test picture of the man in a business suit, facing another who is wearing a uniform and carrying a gun. The first man is gesturing with an agitated expression. Table 3.2 sums up the themes of these stories.

For 64.3 percent of the Japanese but only 38.1 percent of the Americans, the confrontation with authority has strong emotional impact. It generates an atmosphere of guilt, suspicion, protection, or the search for help. Only 35.7 percent of the Japanese but 59.6 percent of the Americans tell a story in which the encounter is trivial, emotionally neutral, or in which the civilian figure is unequivocally superior to the other and in control of the situation.[1]

---

1. As, for example, in a story in which the armed man is not a soldier or a policeman but a security guard employed at the plant of which the civilian is an executive.

Table 3.2. The Man with Gun and Uniform

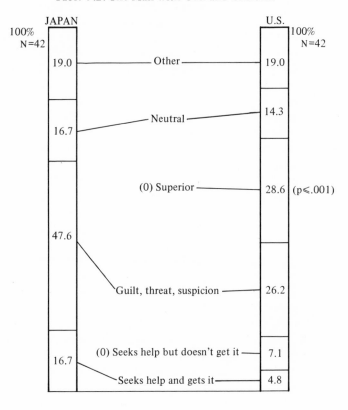

These figures suggest that the image of authority has more emotional impact to the Japanese than it does to the Americans. Authority in itself carries greater weight and more psychological meaning. If we look at the members of both samples who tell stories in which this emotional weight is expressed, we find that almost the same percentage in both groups defines that impact as threatening: the story is about guilt, threat, or suspicion. This category comprises 74 percent of the Japanese subgroup and 69 percent of the American.

Authority for both groups, if it has an emotional meaning, is likely to be frightening or threatening. But it can also be benevolent. Authority can be a refuge, a source of help, a court of last resort. Both Japanese and Americans tell some stories that depict the man gesturing in the picture as seeking help from the soldier-policeman-guard figure. But the outcome of these stories tends to be different for the two groups. In Japanese stories of this kind (16.7 percent of the total), authority is always benevolent and help is always forthcoming. In the American stories (11.9 percent of the total), authority is more likely to refuse help than to give it.

In Japanese political culture, then, authority is more likely to be seen as having a personal emotional impact. It is viewed both as more threatening and as more benevolent. In the American context, authority is cooler, less personally meaningful. It is neither so much a source of danger nor so much a potential source of help. It is *less important*.

That the Americans appear to be less emotionally concerned by formal legal authority is probably related to their de-emphasis of personality. They have sanitized power; this authority-relationship is free from overtones of the personal and the emotional, it is a tool, an abstraction that works according to the rules. With human emotion chilled out, the relationship can be accepted easily. Fur-

thermore, if the classic thesis about American attitudes
toward competition is correct, it is possible that these
Americans are unconcerned about authority because they
accept the conflict implicit in it more easily.[2] If conflict in
general is not threatening, one of the roots of uneasiness
about authority is severed.

For the Japanese, authority is at once more dangerous
and more helpful. Guilt before it can be more threatening,
and the search for help from it can be more rewarding,
because this authority is human and personal. Because it is
emotionally charged, it cannot be accepted dispas-
sionately.

So the reaction is emotional: but what will the emotion
be? For the Japanese there is a predisposition toward the
negative. For formal authority in itself implies a conflict;
and that marks a kind of failure: the law implies the crime,
the policeman the criminal, the soldier the enemy. Legal
coercion is the negation of the organic harmony which is
the Japanese social ideal. Consequently, where for the
American gun and uniform represent conflict and the law,
and these are good, for the Japanese they represent disharmony and crime, and these are bad.

Facing authority, the American expects little and fears
little; the Japanese hopes for much but has deep misgiv-
ings about what he will receive. The American recognizes
that authority implies conflict and accepts this; the Japanese hopes it will be harmonious but is haunted by the
suspicion that it will not be. Because of this, in part, attitudes toward holding power oneself seem to vary too.
Table 3.3 shows the sentence-endings given to: "When
they asked him if he wanted to be the boss, he . . ."

We note that Americans are more likely to say that the
man in the sentence answered yes rather than no. The Japanese are more likely to give an ambivalent conclusion to

2. This thesis is stated, for example, in Margaret Mead, *And Keep Your
Powder Dry* (New York: 1942).

Table 3.3. Do You Want to Be the Boss?

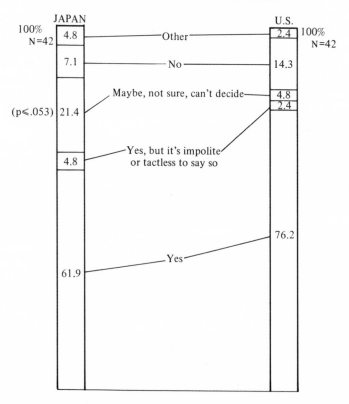

the sentence, suggesting, for example, that he wanted to
be boss but did not think he could, that he wanted to but
did not say so openly, and so on. This ambivalence about
holding power and responsibility is much less marked
among the Americans. A similar pattern is evident in table
3.1 where one American response is, "In a position of
power he feels ambitious for accomplishment" or "he feels
a sense of being chosen, a sense of purpose and mission."
No Japanese give responses such as this, indicating a zest-
ful eagerness to take and use power as "a good thing."

If power is not expected to be exercised well, if it is
threatening, then it is not unambiguously a good. One can
want it then only ambivalently. This seems to be the case
in the Japanese political culture. Part of this ambivalence
is a matter of propriety. Japanese values do not encourage
rivalry, disharmony, and conflict. But the struggle for
power that results when people are in competition for advancement involves all three. A government sub-section
chief (kakaricho) in his thirties summed up this tension
between instinct and form when he commented, "Of
course everyone wants to be boss some day. But you must
never admit this openly."

Ambition is encouraged and praised in the American
context. In the Japanese world many words for ambition
(yabo, yashin) have connotations of scheming for advancement, of being an upstart, of intrigue, of social climbing.
The American teacher Clark, who spent three monts at
Sapporo University in the 1870's left an imperishable mark
in popular mythology with his famous exhortation, "Boys,
be ambitious!" But what he is considered to have said in
Japanese is "have great thoughts," (taishi). For the Americans power is expected to be used "well," and if, to the individual subject to it, it is not a source of benevolence, it is
also less likely to be a source of threat. It is a tool, to be
used for a task; therefore one can want it wholeheartedly.
If power is bad, it is bad to want it; if it is good, it is all

right to want it. Thus, Americans continue to believe that every boy should dream of growing up to be President, even if only of General Motors.

Because authority differs in character, it calls forth different responses from those subject to it. Table 3.4 summarizes sentence completions for: "When his superior ordered him to do it, he . . ."

The overwhelming American response is "he did it." Here there is nothing problematic, nothing personal; the relationship is automatic and acceptable. One man gives another a command, the other executes it: the basic relationship of hierarchy. But the American response is purged of all the emotional elements that make hierarchy desirable or undesirable. It is a response that sees hierarchy as impersonal and reasonable: reasonable *because* impersonal, or *inasmuch as* impersonal.

Americans are more concerned with following the rules in this hierarchical relationship, with just "doing it," because following the rules sterilizes and sanitizes the confrontation of superior and subordinate. The confrontation is made feasible by ritualizing and depersonalizing, streamlining out the personal element, and thus minimizing potential conflict. Just be obedient, just follow the rules. That's all that's required to create the rarefication of the human atmosphere, the thinning out of the emotions, with which the Americans seem to be most at ease.

The American responses to authority are cut and dried, more formalistic than those of the "formal" Japanese,[3] because these responses, for the Americans, really are thin and denatured. What do you feel in the presence of the boss? Nothing particular—just that one ought to obey. But the Japanese emotions are not so stifled. For the Japanese authority is personal and more therefore is expected and more feared from it. Where the underlying emotion, the

3. As Ruth Benedict, among many others, observed: *The Chrysanthemum and the Sword: Patterns of Japanese Culture* (Tokyo: 1954).

Table 3.4. When His Superior Ordered Him to Do It

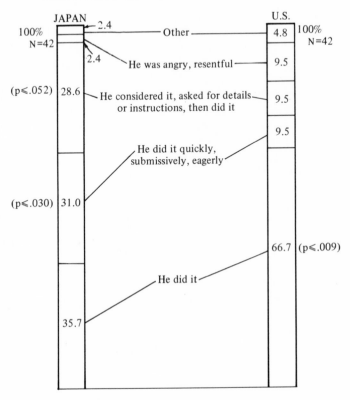

JAPAN

U.S.

100% N=42

100% N=42

2.4 — Other — 4.8

2.4 — He was angry, resentful — 9.5

(p≤.052) 28.6 — He considered it, asked for details or instructions, then did it — 9.5

9.5

He did it quickly, submissively, eagerly

(p≤.030) 31.0

66.7 (p≤.009)

He did it

35.7

fear, love, anger of the personal element, is vivid and
thick, then ritual and ceremony are needed to contain it.
For the Japanese, ritual and form are ever-present and
ever-necessary to defend against emotion. And in a form of
circular causation, ritual and ceremony in their turn feed
the hungry, nervous search for the *true* emotion that the
formalists and ritualizers feel must lie beneath. For the
Americans, outer forms are perhaps less necessary because
the inner forces are less unruly; their souls are more con-
ventional, they need conventions of behavior less.

They can take authority for granted; the Japanese are
less inclined to. The Japanese pattern is different. The
relation to authority is more often personalized by choice.
It is not enough to say "he was ordered to do it and he did
it." The recipient of the Japanese order does it quickly,
eagerly, submissively, obsequiously, with all his might,
thoroughly, and gladly. He makes it a personal act, one
that takes on the coloring of the emotional relationship of
the two men, the once commanding, the other obeying. Or
the relationship may be personalized by these respondents
through adding flesh and substance to the interchange between superior and inferior. The inferior does not just
carry out his order. He considers it, he asks for details, he
discusses how best to go about it, he checks the problematic angles, and so forth. This not only humanizes the relationship of hierarchy but it also allows the inferior to share
in the authority that is exercised. In however small a way,
by discussing the order given, he has a hand in formulat-
ing it. The American relationship is impersonal and clearcut. The Japanese relationship is personal and therefore
loses a degree of clarity.

Because authority is impersonal, cool, and less threatening—because it is expected to be responsible although not
benevolent—it seems easier for the American than for the
Japanese to relate to it and to deal with it. One of the
Hanfmann–Getzels survey items, the story of the unrea-

sonable new department head, illustrates this aspect of the hierarchical relationship:

A new department head is appointed who makes consistently unreasonable demands on his subordinates. If you faced this problem, which of the following courses of action would you choose?

a. Go to the department head and tell him frankly that his way of doing things is not the way they are done here.

b. Appear to accept his orders, but resist by a program of covert non-compliance.

c. Do the best you can under the circumstances.

d. Complain to the department head's superior.

e. Adopt a wait-and-see attitude, feeling that this is not a problem for the department as a whole but for each individual.

f. Other.

The overwhelmingly popular Japanese response to this question is "a." Because of the wording in "e," it is implied that this is a group decision in which the new department head is confronted by a united front which presents him with a nonnegotiable ultimatum.

The most popular American response, on the other hand, is "f," "other." Forty percent of the Americans wrote in here essentially the same suggestion: speak to the department head confidentially on an individual basis and let him know tactfully what the problem is. A possible explanation of this pattern of response is that a low-key approach is possible for the Americans because authority is expected to be reasonable. Nothing but confrontation can succeed for the Japanese because authority is personalistic and there is no assurance that the personality of the leader is reasonable. The odds are in the other direction: if reason is impersonal, the personal element is essentially nonreasonable.

Table 3.5. The Unreasonable New Department Head

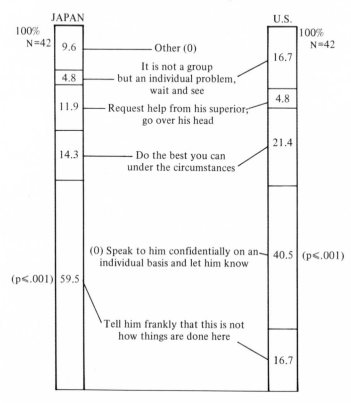

JAPAN

100%
N=42

9.6 ——————— Other (0)

It is not a group
4.8 — but an individual problem,
wait and see

11.9 — Request help from his superior;
go over his head

14.3 ——————— Do the best you can
under the circumstances

(0) Speak to him confidentially on an
individual basis and let him know

(p≤.001) 59.5

Tell him frankly that this is not
how things are done here

U.S.

100%
N=42

16.7

4.8

21.4

40.5 (p≤.001)

16.7

The Americans depersonalize authority, the Japanese hope it will be personal. The Americans expect little from it and react to it matter-of-factly and mechanically, the Japanese hope and apprehend much from it and are consequently hindered in dealing with it openly and easily. For the Japanese, authority depends on the group's legitimation; for the Americans it is a matter of individual confronting individual, and this confrontation is guided, ordered, and sanitized by the formal rules.

Warmth and trust are valued more highly in the hierarchical relationship of Japan than in that of the United States. But the personalism that erects these values makes them harder to attain in practice.

This uncertainty about the reactions of authority is visible also in the responses to: "When he was given an order he knew was wrong, he . . ." (see table 3.6). The pattern is roughly similar for Japanese and Americans, except for the significantly larger number of Japanese who do not answer or who give trivial, nonclassifiable, or evasive answers. It is more difficult in the Japanese context to formulate an appropriate response.[4]

Authority in Japan, we have seen, is more likely to seem corrupt, or ineffectual, or arrogant; yet also more likely to be personal. It is more ambiguous morally, and its desirability is less clear. It is harder to oppose and opposition is more likely to involve confrontation. Finally, it is less secure.

Table 3.7 shows the stories told about the TAT pic-

4. For example, "One ought to refuse." But this "ought" is a device for refusing to imagine an action: it transposes the situation from the actual to the theoretical. Or, "He feels silent scorn." Here, silence reconciles the conflict: the order is carried out but one's personal honor is satisfied by unspoken scorn for the superior. Because the Japanese demand a more intimate and personal authority, it is harder, not easier, to speak frankly to it. An open confrontation is avoided because too much is at stake. Compliance is public, scorn is private; the order "ought" to be queried in theory; but in actuality the contradictions of power, when they appear glaringly, as here, are more likely to be veiled or ignored if possible.

Table 3.6. When He Was Given an Order He Knew Was Wrong

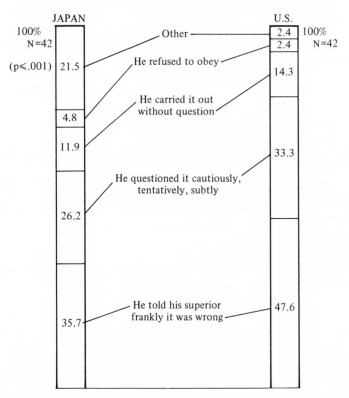

Table 3.7. The Man in the Door of the Conference Room

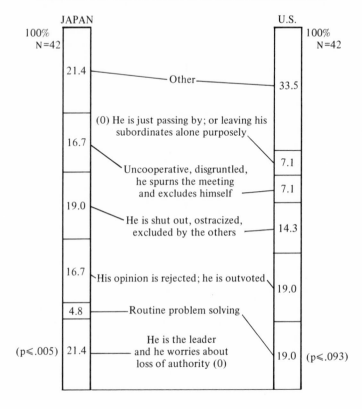

JAPAN

100%
N=42

21.4

16.7

19.0

16.7

4.8

(p≤.005) 21.4

Other

(0) He is just passing by; or leaving his
subordinates alone purposely

Uncooperative, disgruntled,
he spurns the meeting
and excludes himself

He is shut out, ostracized,
excluded by the others

His opinion is rejected; he is outvoted

Routine problem solving

He is the leader
and he worries about
loss of authority (0)

U.S.

100%
N=42

33.5

7.1

7.1

14.3

19.0

19.0 (p≤.093)

ture of the man standing in the door of the conference room. More than half of the Japanese and 30.4 percent of the Americans tell stories of ostracism, rejection, or exclusion. In addition to these, there is another type of exclusion narrative that is told by 21.4 percent of the Japanese but by none of the Americans. This is the story of the leader who fears that his men are banding together to defy his authority.

This trait follows logically from the forms of legitimation characteristic of each culture. If authority rests on compliance with prescriptive rules and on satisfactory performance of a specific task, as for the Americans, then it is possible to be fairly sure about how secure one's authority is. If the rules are followed and the task is done, then authority is stable. But if personalistic factors are the basic legitimators of authority, then the power-holder can never be secure. This is because any personal relationship has two sides and the leader can be responsible for only one. He can never control or be certain of the sufficiency of the relationship as a whole and thus can never be assured of his legitimacy and the stability of his tenure in power.

Because power for the Japanese is more personalistic, it is more ambivalent. Because it is more ambivalent, it is more dangerous and threatening. Because it is more dangerous, it is more important. Thus, it is not surprising to find that, being more concerned about authority, the Japanese are more authoritarian.

Table 3.8 shows Japanese and American scores on the short form of the Rokeach Dogmatism Scale. Each numerical score represents the mean of the groups' agreement or disagreement with one of the ten statements on a scale where 1 means "disagree strongly," 6 means "agree strongly" and 3.5 represents indifference.

On a scale that purports to measure stereotypical thinking, exclusiveness, pessimism about human nature, and authoritarianism, the American group scores highest on

Table 3.8. The Rokeach Dogmatism Scale

Item	Japanese Mean	American Mean	Significance
1. The worst crime a person can commit is to attack publicly the people who believe in the same thing he does.	4.214	3.000	p ≤ .003
2. It is often desirable to reserve judgment about what's going on until one has a chance to hear the opinions of those one respects.	2.762	4.667	p ≤ .001
3. Fundamentally, the world we live in is a pretty lonely place.	3.548	3.214	p ≤ .382 (not significant)
4. In the history of mankind there have probably been just a handful of really great thinkers.	5.167	3.500	p ≤ .001
5. In the long run the best way to live is to pick friends and associates whose tastes and beliefs are the same as one's own.	4.548	2.805	p ≤ .001
6. Most people just don't know what's good for them.	4.190	3.024	p ≤ .001
7. Once I get wound up in a heated discussion I just can't stop.	4.190	2.976	p ≤ .001
8. In this complicated world of ours the only way we can know what is going on is to rely on leaders or experts who can be trusted.	3.643	2.659	p ≤ .009

Item	Japanese Mean	American Mean	Significance
9. A person who thinks primarily of his own happiness is beneath contempt.	4.500	3.146	p ≤ .001
10. While I don't like to admit this even to myself, I sometimes have the ambition to become a great man.	4.143	4.238	p over .5 (not significant)

two items, the Japanese on eight. The two items on which the Americans score high are congruent with the complex of cultural traits we have described before. That is, when Americans more than Japanese feel it is desirable to reserve judgment until one has a chance to hear the opinions of those one respects, they may be expressing a belief in moderate rationality that suits better with prescriptive than personalistic decision-making procedures.[5] And when Americans more than Japanese admit to the ambition to become a great man, they vouch for the relative innocence of authority that we have noted in their political culture. For Americans, authority is good and it is right to want it. For the Japanese, it is ambivalent and dangerous: one must be concerned about it, but it is dubious to admit publicly to a desire for "greatness" in its possession.

5. It is possible too that some of the Japanese respondents may be trying to give a "good" answer in stressing independent and autonomous thinking rather than the consensus, group-oriented stereotype so often attributed to them.

4: Relations of Equality

Politics is not only the vertical relationship of unequals but also the horizontal bond of equals. Power, which is the stuff of politics, is expressed in hierarchies of coercion or command but it is generated by organization, coordination and cooperation and these processes take place among equals as well as among unequals.

An important part of the political culture of a people, then, is found in the answers to such questions as "What is a good peer like?" "What is a bad peer like?" "What is a friend?" "Where and what are the dangers of social life?" "Where and what is the help against these dangers?" "What is the best stance to adopt toward one's social world?" In short, how does one live in groups?

What one likes and what one dislikes in one's companions or colleagues form an empirically operative standard of virtue and vice for a society. Japanese and Americans define these virtues and vices in different ways.

Table 4.1 shows their respective conclusions to the unfinished sentence, "What I like best in him is . . ." On no single quality specified is there a statistically significant difference in the frequency for the two groups but the overall trend shows a striking difference in emphasis. There are two sorts of virtues described. One set consists of what might be called the "nice guy" qualities: open, friendly, cheerful, warm, easygoing, and humorous. Of the American responses, 57.1 percent fall into this category but only 33.3 percent of the Japanese. Another set of quali-

Table 4.1. What I Like Best in Him

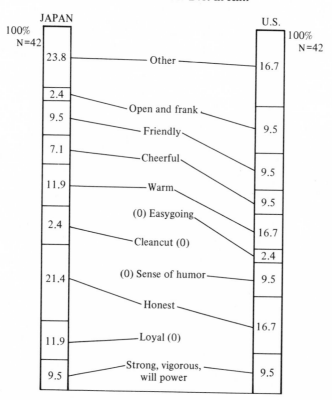

ties is marked by a concern for "character," for moral virtue in a more classic sense: honesty, loyalty, strength of will. Traits of this latter sort are cited by 42.8 percent of the Japanese but only 26.2 percent of the Americans. Americans seem to rate their peers by how much fun they are to be with, Japanese by how well they adhere to moral standards. Americans respect nice guys, Japanese respect sterling characters.

Is this impression confirmed by their dislikes as well? Table 4.2 charts their first-ranked responses to the question, "In your own experience what sort of people are hardest to work with? Please list three characteristics of this sort of person." At the individual trait level, Japanese are significantly more likely to describe the "bad" peer as uncooperative or sly. At the overall level, traits that make a person unpleasant to be with as a companion, the opposite of the "nice guy" qualities—rigid, gossipy, will not listen to others, cool, overemotional—are suggested by 59.6 percent of the Americans but only by 23.9 percent of the Japanese. On the other hand, bad qualities that involve bad morals or wrong action as well as an unpleasant personality—sly, uncooperative, selfish, egotistic—are suggested by 64.3 percent of the Japanese but only by 33.6 percent of the Americans.

For the Americans, virtue and vice are qualities of personality. They have to do with how pleasant or unpleasant one is as a companion. They are essentially *cosmetic.* For the Japanese, virtue and vice are qualities of action or responsibility toward others. They are not a matter of how one looks but of how one acts. They are ultimately serious in a way that the American equivalents are not. They have to do with the quality of one's relationship to the society around him. The greatest virtue is honesty and the greatest vice is lack of cooperation.

Japanese take social relations more seriously than Americans do. One is judged by his peers on his character, on

Table 4.2. The Bad Peer

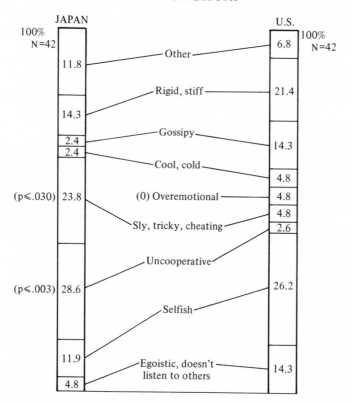

how well he lives up to the demands of his role in his group. For Americans, one is judged by personality, by how much fun he is to be with. The different standards reflect the differing weight the two societies place on peer-group relations.

This same dichotomy is expressed with an ironic reversal of emphasis, in the responses of the two groups to the unfinished sentence, "A really close friend is one who . . ." (table 4.3). For the Japanese, a really close friend is one to whom you can talk, in whom you can confide. For the Americans, a really close friend is one who is self-sacrificing, trustworthy, and loyal. What has happened here? The Japanese, erecting the stern demands of "character" as the standard of virtue for their peers in general, seek in a close friend not character but human warmth, communication, personality. The Americans, who seek in a peer in general only the nice guy virtues, reserve for a close friend the requirements of character.

There is in both cases a split between what is valued in the public relationship and what is reserved for the private. For the Americans, the cosmetic, the personal, the nice guy aspect is public; moral character is private. For the Japanese, character is public and human feeling is private. Character is more serious than personality, morality more serious than a pleasant air of bonhomie. It follows then that for Americans it is the private relationship, the bond of two individuals that is most important; and for the Japanese, the most important is the public relationship, the common links that unite many into a group.[1]

The American emphasis on the self and the Japanese emphasis on the social nexus are seen in table 4.4 also: "He was most afraid of . . ." Half of the Americans suggest that inner fears are the most important—one's own

1. This thesis finds classic formulation in Hajime Nakamura, *Ways of Thinking of Eastern Peoples: India, China, Tibet, Japan* (Honolulu: 1964), pp. 407–530.

Table 4.3. A Really Close Friend

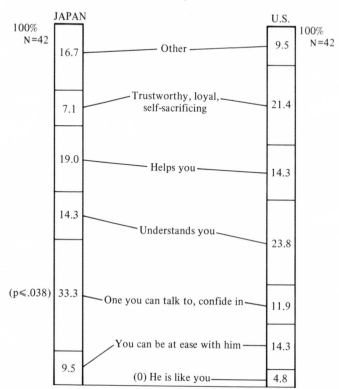

JAPAN

U.S.

100%
N=42

100%
N=42

16.7 — Other — 9.5

7.1 — Trustworthy, loyal, self-sacrificing — 21.4

19.0 — Helps you — 14.3

14.3 — Understands you — 23.8

(p≤.038) 33.3 — One you can talk to, confide in — 11.9

You can be at ease with him — 14.3

9.5

(0) He is like you — 4.8

Table 4.4. He Was Most Afraid of . . .

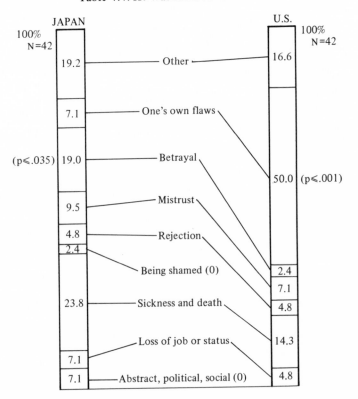

failures, flaws, and inadequacies. "He was most afraid of stumbling in a crisis." "He was most afraid of failing to measure up." "He was most afraid of being late." The most important category for the Japanese concerns the action of others—being betrayed, being shamed, being rejected. If we divide the world of fears and dangers into four areas, the Japanese rank them:

1; the actions of others	35.7%
2) impersonal (sickness, death, job loss)	30.9%
3) other or abstract	26.1%
4) one's own flaws	7.1%

and the Americans rank them:

1) one's own flaws	50.0%
2) impersonal (sickness, death, job loss)	19.1%
3) the actions of others	16.7%
4) other or abstract	16.7%

What one fears is a good indication of what one considers important. Japanese fears are external, American fears internal. The outer social world is important to the Japanese. For Americans, it is the inner world of the individual that is important.

What is feared is one indicator of cultural attitudes. How the fear is dealt with is another. Political culture is shaped not only by the problems that people envisage, but also by the modes of coping with them that they are accustomed to employ. There are two kinds of threats, internal and external. How Japanese and Americans handle the external threat is shown in table 4.5: "When one is frightened by something, the best thing to do is . . ."

The two cultures are very much alike in their handling of external danger. The most favored solution is autonomous consideration (plan/analyze or pray/meditate): 54.8 percent of the Americans, 35.7 percent of the Japanese. Second ranked is endurance or inaction ("the best

Table 4.5. When One Is Frightened by Something, the Best Thing to Do Is . . .

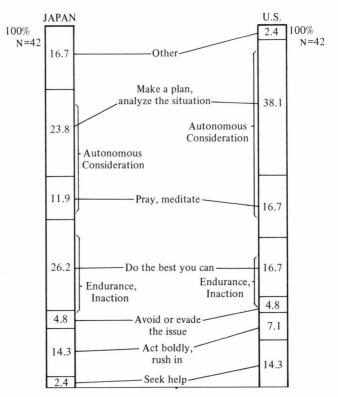

JAPAN

100%
N=42

16.7 — Other

23.8

Autonomous
Consideration

11.9 — Pray, meditate

26.2 — Do the best you can

Endurance,
Inaction

4.8 — Avoid or evade
the issue

14.3 — Act boldly,
rush in

2.4 — Seek help

Make a plan,
analyze the situation

U.S.

2.4
100%
N=42

38.1

Autonomous
Consideration

16.7

16.7

Endurance,
Inaction

4.8

7.1

14.3

Table 4.6. When Troubled, What One Usually Does Is . . .

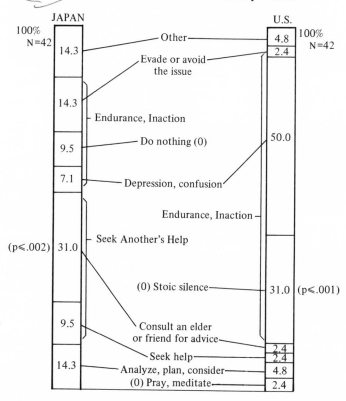

you can," avoidance or evasion): 31.0 percent of the Japanese, 21.5 percent of the Americans. A third strategy, "act
boldly, dash in and grapple with it" is suggested by 14.3
percent of the Japanese and 7.1 percent of the Americans.
Seeking the help of others is suggested by 2.4 percent of
the Japanese and 14.3 percent of the Americans.

The only difference in emphasis is the relatively minor
one that Americans rank seeking help higher than quick
bold action and Japanese reverse this ranking. It is possible that this difference in shading is the result of the Japanese concern with strength of character (not appearing to
be weak or cowardly). For both cultures, in any case, the
external threat is handled primarily by autonomous analysis and consideration.

When we look at the inner threat—"When troubled,
what one usually does is . . ."—the picture is quite different. This is apparent in the data of table 4.6. The two
cultures suggest widely variant strategies for dealing with
personal problems. The most generally advocated Japanese strategy is to seek help. To consult an elder or a
trusted friend for advice is the most common answer to the
dilemma. Its predominance in Japanese culture over
American culture, judging from this data, is marked. The
American solution is inactive endurance. Fifty percent of
the Americans complete the sentence by indicating simply
the likelihood of depression or confusion, and 31 percent
advocate bearing one's troubles in stoic silence. This latter
tactic is suggested by none of the Japanese and its American predominance is highly significant.

The ranking of modes of coping with care and trouble,
then, are for the Japanese:

1) seek help	40.5%	
2) inactive endurance	30.9%	
3) autonomous consideration	14.3%	

and for the Americans:

    1) inactive endurance   83.4%
    2) autonomous consideration   7.2%
    3) seek help   4.8%

The more outward orientation of the Japanese to the social world means that when they have private problems they can get help for them from others. The American relative devaluation of the social nexus means that in the face of private problems there is little help to be expected from outside.

The security of the Japanese social matrix and the insecurity of the American loneliness are illustrated in the responses to one of the Hanfman-Getzels hypothetical situations:

> Someone gets the feeling that other people are talking about him behind his back. If he enters a room, the conversation stops or the subject is changed. Finally he can't stand it any longer and approaches his colleagues. But the conversation stops and the atmosphere cools. If you were the person in question, which of the following would you do?
>
> a) Ask frankly what the problem is and if it is your own fault, correct it.
>
> b) Approach one of your colleagues in a private discussion and ask for advice.
>
> c) Examine your own conduct privately and try to correct whatever could be the problem.
>
> d) Continue to ignore the situation.
>
> e) Other.

In this dilemma, Americans are much more likely (see table 4.7) to envisage approaching another individual privately and Japanese are much more likely to ask about the problem openly. The American emphasis on the individual condemns the man with a problem to an individual solution. The Japanese emphasis on the group means

Table 4.7. They Talk about Him behind His back

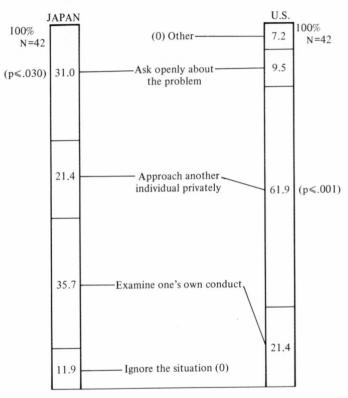

JAPAN
100%
N=42

(p≤.030)

31.0 — Ask openly about the problem

21.4 — Approach another individual privately

35.7 — Examine one's own conduct

11.9 — Ignore the situation (0)

(0) Other

U.S.
100%
N=42

7.2

9.5

61.9 (p≤.001)

21.4

among other things that the group can be therapeutic and that private problems can have public solutions.

The Japanese, in this particular story, recognize the real existence of a group, which excludes the hero of the story and has a right to do so. The hero, however, has also a right to be readmitted after he clears the air by confessing his faults and correcting them. To correct the situation, he approaches the group as a whole.

The Americans are not so likely to recognize the group as a legitimate entity with legitimate claims to make on the individual. How then can they appeal to it openly? The problem is an individual problem and the solution to it involves only individuals, because there is no group supposed to have existential weight and important prerogatives of its own.

Since the group is more important and more real to our Japanese contributors, they are inclined to bring the problem to it as the proper forum. Their American counterparts recognize the group neither as entity, nor as forum, nor as solution. They fail to see the group as the Japanese do, not because Americans are less perceptive but because the American group is less real.

The most basic cultural attitudes toward the reality of the social group are revealed in the answers to unfinished sentences like, "He is most careful in his relations with others of . . ." (table 4.8).

Here the two cultures stand revealed as essentially similar in their attitudes toward social intercourse. There are three strategies governing our interaction with others. We may be manipulative (concerned for ourselves), benevolent (concerned for the other), or isolative (concerned to avoid involvement). Exactly one third of both Americans and Japanese recommends manipulative strategies ("know what the other is thinking" and "make a good impression"). Almost exactly another third recommends benevolent attitudes (love, trust, sincerity, harmony, avoidance of

Table 4.8. He Is Most Careful in His Relations with Others of . . .

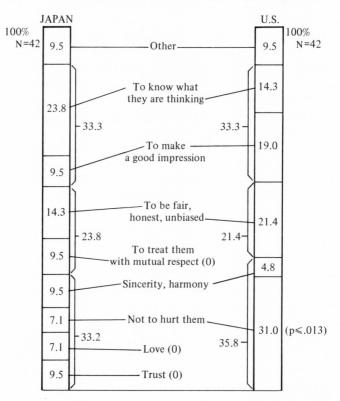

harm to others). A little more than 20 percent in each culture adopts the stand-off strategy of isolation: mutual respect, honesty, fairness, unbiasedness.

There are statistically significant differences between the patterns of response of Americans and Japanese, but they are at a sublevel of meaning. Thus, within the category of the benevolent attitude in general, Japanese answers stress harmony, trust, and love; American answers are almost exclusively of the sort "not to hurt others."

The Japanese concept of benevolence here expressed is a social, active, and mutually involved one. It takes two to harmonize, to trust, or to love. The American concept is isolated, uninvolved, individual, and separatist: not hurting others may mean only the avoidance of an active relationship. In this question we appear to reach one limit of Japanese-American cultural variation (active, social or passive, individual altruism) and to go beyond it to what seems a common basis of humanity (the uniform distribution of manipulative, benevolent, and isolative attitudes).

This pattern is corroborated by another sentence completion item: "It is sometimes good to hide your true feelings about others because . . ." In this case (table 4.9) the manipulative strategy is envisioned by 35.7 percent of each sample ("to get ahead," "to avoid unpleasantness"). The stand-off attitude is advocated by 16.7 percent of each ("it is proper," "you might be mistaken"). And 23.8 percent of the Japanese and 38.1 percent of the Americans adopt a benevolent attitude ("don't hurt the other's feelings"). Here again the significant differences are found not at the level of gross attitudinal orientations, but at the shallower level of the justifications given for adopting those attitudes. So the stand-off attitude is recommended by Japanese "because it is proper" and "because it is correct." As one bureaucratic respondent wrote, "Hiding one's feelings has always been considered a good thing in Japan from ancient times." And the same attitude is rec-

Table 4.9. It Is Sometimes Good to Hide Your True Feelings
About Others because . . .

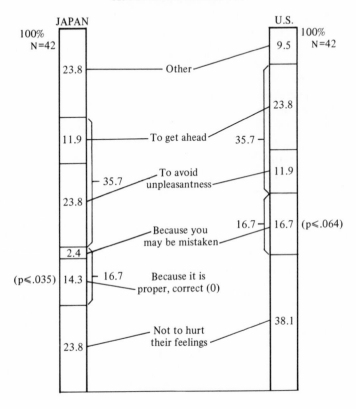

ommended by Americans "because you might be mistaken." In both cultures there are good reasons not to be entirely honest and open. But in the one, the reasons for action and the consequences of failure are social; in the other they are individual.

In this examination of the relations of equality, of the individual with his peers, we have found a consistent difference of emphasis between the Japanese and American cultures which has to do with the relative value of the individual and the social. Americans and Japanese both value moral character and both value the nice guy qualities. But they value them in different places and in different contexts.

Virtue and vice in the peer in general are defined by the American as "personality" qualities, the qualities of being a "nice guy." For the Japanese, they are qualities of character, of adherence to moral standards. In a close friend, on the other hand, Americans value qualities of character whereas the Japanese value the intimate qualities of personal communication. If moral character is more serious, important, and basic, in some sense, then, we can conclude that the important relationship for Americans is the private one and for the Japanese, the public.

Just as Americans seem to value the individual and Japanese the social context, so what Americans fear is individual (the failure of self) and what Japanese fear is social (the ill-doing of others). Not only the prevailing fears but the remedies for them reveal this difference in emphasis. When troubled, the Americans seem to have little alternative to silent and stoic individual suffering. The Japanese have access to help from others, just as they fear the harm that others may do.

At a most basic level, the orientations to social life of Americans and Japanese are remarkably similar. A relatively constant proportion of both populations chooses benevolent, manipulative, or isolative strategies in intercourse with their fellows. But the justifications for these strategies and the forms the strategies take differ along the lines suggested earlier. Social uninvolvement is defended by the Japanese because it is dictated by the rules of propriety; by the Americans because it serves one's self-interest. Benevolence for Japanese is active, social, involved, and mutual; for Americans it is passive, individual, uninvolved, and one-sided. The manipulative attitude needs no justification in either culture. Neither does it appear to differ in kind from one society to the other.

5: Relations of Conflict

If cooperation and coordination are only possible among equals, it is true that conflict also presupposes equality. Only with the cessation of conflict and the fixation of its outcome does hierarchy become possible. Attitudes toward conflict and harmony, like those toward equality and hierarchy, are at the heart of political culture.

Since these two dimensions are intimately related, it is not surprising to find that Japanese and Americans differ notably with regard to the sources of conflict, their attitudes toward its open expression, and the ways in which they characteristically engage in it. "What makes a man most angry": definitions of the sources of anger and conflict for the two cultures are outlined in table 5.1.

For the Japanese, the overwhelmingly preponderant cause for anger is to be victimized by someone else. To be betrayed, to be mistrusted, to be insulted, to be humiliated, to be cheated: these are the origins of conflict. What one resents most is damage to one's image of oneself. "Victimization" of this kind accounts for 85.5 percent of Japanese responses but only 19.2 percent of American. For the Americans, the greatest single cause of anger is not to get one's way—the disobedience or resistance of others (26.2 percent $p \leqslant .002$). A close second is one's own faults (16.7 percent, $p \leqslant .035$).

The Japanese of our sample appear to be at ease with themselves but at odds with other men. The source of conflict is in the other person. They are hetero-aitiastics,

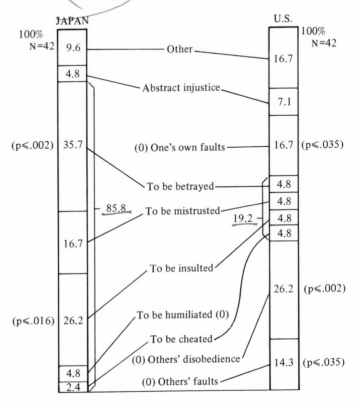

Table 5.1. What Makes a Man Most Angry

other-blamers. The Americans are in conflict with themselves and unsatisfied with themselves, but relatively at ease with others. They are auto-aitiastics, self-blamers.

Even where the Americans appear to be angry at others, it is in a context different from that of the Japanese group. The latter are angry when others shame them, betray them, distrust them, or leave them out. The American is angry when his authority is ignored. What really angers him here is that the rules are being broken. He has a "right" to be obeyed and to give orders and a "legitimate" expectation that his orders will be carried out. Both the Japanese and the Americans are men of authority; but the authority of the American is by statute and that of the Japanese is by mutual agreement. The Americans, with their universalist expectations about the virtue of rules, are angry when they are broken. The Japanese since, they recognize them less, lay less weight on their violation.

What seems to anger the Japanese is damage to their self-image; what seems to anger Americans is damage to their self-interest. Japanese anger is born as a response to what is seen as an attack or a victimization by others. American anger is born out of impatience with one's own faults or the resistance of others. Americans see themselves as dominant and are angry when they fail to maintain dominance, whether because of their own insufficiency or because of others' resistance. Japanese see themselves as victims and their anger is the anger of the man who is injured, not the one who fails to get his own way.[1]

Japanese and Americans get angry for different reasons. They also regard the open expression of that anger very differently. Table 5.2 shows their responses to the fourth TAT picture, that of the two groups in conflict. The stories

1. This trait seems a form of what Maruyama has called *higaisha-ishiki*, and its appearance in our data a corroboration of his intuitive concept. See *Nihon No Shiso* (Tokyo: 1961), pp. 142–143.

Table 5.2. Groups in Conflict

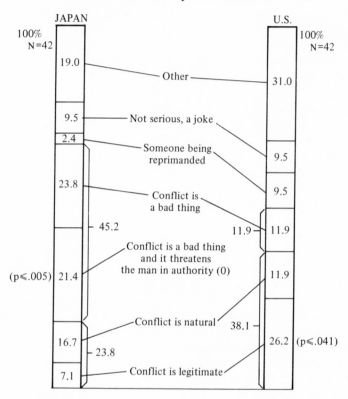

told to describe this scene had to include some kind of explanation for the separation of the two groups of men, their huddled whispers, the air of concern and expectation with which they gaze upon each other. In this picture, conflict and aggression are only lightly veiled.

But many of both groups do not see it as a conflict situation. For some it is a picture of a game; for others, the telling of crude stories; it may be secret good news or the new secretary's pretty legs. Most Japanese and Americans, however, do recognize conflict in the picture and most tell a story describing the conflict which implies a moral judgment. Either the conflict is good and legitimate or it is bad and ought to be suppressed.

For 45.2 percent of the Japanese, open conflict is seen as a bad thing. Only 11.9 percent of the Americans respond in this way. For 38.1 percent of the Americans, conflict is seen as natural or legitimate. Only 23.8 percent of the Japanese respond thus. Cultural attitudes toward the open expression of anger and conflict are thus diametrically opposed. A plurality of Americans believes conflict is natural and legitimate and a small minority believes that it is bad. A plurality of Japanese believes that conflict is dangerous and bad and a small minority believes that it is legitimate. Furthermore, in an interesting demonstration of the importance of the maintenance of hierarchy to the Japanese respondents, 21.4 percent of them specify that the conflict in the picture is bad because it threatens the authority of the leader; none of the Americans makes this suggestion.

By the Japanese the scene is often interpreted as representing cabals, plots, factional strife, and devious underground struggles. For the Americans, the actors are typically management and labor teams negotiating, teams of executives locked in practice conflict in a management game, or lawyers and witnesses at a Senate subcommittee hearing. The conflict is open, apparent, and taken for granted. It is not condemned.

It may be that the American sanitization of emotion has succeeded in cleansing aggressive action of personal feelings to such an extent that it can be ritualized, dramatized, and brought into the open. Just as the Americans have attempted to pasteurize authority by subjecting it to rules so that it can be safely taken for granted, so they have attempted to purify and to denature aggressive impulses, making it possible for these to drive the engines of socially institutionalized conflict without explosion.

For the Japanese respondents anger and aggression seem too strong, too personal, too uncontrollable to be allowed to appear in public. Even when institutionalized, conflict is dangerous. The ordered conflict of the strike demonstration may burst into murder and violence and the debate on the Diet floor may degenerate into fisticuffs. All parties to a dispute know this and they agree in condemning the appearance of disagreement. Anger and aggression are too real to be invoked in everyday differences of interest. Difference of interest, then, must be hidden.[2]

Anger is ubiquitous in any society, but Americans and Japanese are roused to it differently, handle it differently, and guide it in different directions. For the Japanese, anger is the result of others' actions: betrayal, shame, deceit. For the Americans, it is a result of one's own failures or a breach of the abstract rules defining one's "rights." For the Japanese, rage is vivid, immediate, and real; for the Americans, it is muffled, denied, and sanitized.

The aggressive energy of the Japanese is directed outward at others, not openly but in the form of the striving for advantage, for revenge, to find the opponent's weak point, to get the upper hand. The aggressive energy of the

2. This is a classic theme in studies of Japanese culture. Two analyses of the consequences of these attitudes are Ishida Takeshi, "The Development of Interest Groups and the Pattern of Political Modernization in Japan" in *Political Development in Modern Japan*, ed. Robert Ward (Princeton, N.J.: 1968), and Kurt Steiner, "Popular Political Participation and Political Development in Japan: The Rural Level," ibid., p. 243.

Americans is self-directed or sublimated into the ritualized conflict that accompanies the working of government and industry and every organized social endeavor in American culture.[3]

The Americans can afford to have their conflict-games out in the open, perhaps because they have more stringent inner controls over their angers. The Japanese have less rigid inward controls, but outward social control prohibits the open conflict and the admitted aggression. This social control makes impossible the ritual combats and institutionalized battles the Americans, with their emotional blades buttoned and blunted, delight to engage in.

If the relative importance of various sources of anger differs from culture to culture, as well as the perceived legitimacy of open conflict, can we predict what will be the expression of anger in a given situation? Table 5.3 shows the outline of responses to the situation: "When someone bothers him . . ."

The Americans are much more likely to avoid the source of anger; the Japanese are more likely to be angry, annoyed, or to seek revenge. The preference ranking looks like this for the former:

Avoid	43.2%
Attack	23.9%
Analyze	9.5%

and this for the latter:

Attack	31.0%
Avoid	28.6%
Analyze	23.8%

Seven percent of the Americans, but none of the Japanese, cut through the Gordian knot with the fine simplicity of

3. This analysis follows the theoretical pattern suggested by Heinz Hartmann, Ernst Kris, and Rudolph M. Loewenstein in "Notes on the Theory of Aggression" in *Psychological Issues*, vol. 4, no. 2, monograph 14, *Papers in Psychoanalytic Psychology* (New York: 1964), pp. 56–85.

Table 5.3. When Someone Bothers Him . . .

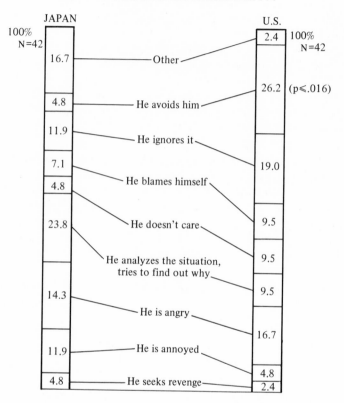

"when someone annoys him he tells him so" (subcategory of "analyze").

There are here then two very distinct patterns of dealing with aggression. The typical American contributor devitalizes aggression as he devitalizes and sanitizes other forms of obtrusive emotion. He "ignores it." He "doesn't care." He may not turn the other cheek but he ignores the pinprick of the mosquito bite on the first. And if this attitude should fail, there is another which should work. Tell the other who annoys you that he does so and the annoyance will stop.

To his Japanese counterpart, these American strategies of handling interpersonal irritation must seem either the plodding insensitivity of clods with no sense of honor or the clumsy destructiveness of the bull in the china shop.

For the Japanese, even the pinprick of annoyance from someone else cannot easily be ignored. The anger is vividly and immediately felt. It cannot be stifled or hidden as by the American and it must be turned in or out. Mostly, it is turned out. Annoy one of our Japanese respondents at your peril: he will "find a counter-strategy," he will "have his revenge." With a touchy feudal sense of personal honor, he will get his own back. Not now, for revenge may be long delayed. But some response—either an angry inner introspection ("it must have been my fault? What did *I* do?") or a meticulous plan for evening the outward balance of annoyance and advantage—must be found.

But the response cannot be to bring the problem into the open. If the American tends to believe this will solve everything—get it out in the light and the problem will reveal its own solution—the Japanese knows better. When he annoys you, tell him so? This is destructive and irresponsible. The initial annoyance, brought into the light, though it might wither and shrivel in the American culture, would spread and thrive and complicate itself in the Japanese.

Paradoxically, Americans, who seem to believe that open conflict is legitimate, avoid it; and Japanese, who feel that conflict is bad, are more prone to give in to it. Further evidence from table 5.4 confirms the paradox and helps elucidate it.

"When someone insults him . . ." carries the provocation to anger to a new and higher level. But the relative weight of attack and avoidance in the Japanese and American samples remains much the same:

Japan:	Attack	57.2
	Avoid	28.5
	Analyze	0.0
U.S.:	Attack	45.3
	Avoid	40.4
	Analyze	9.5

The Americans are relatively more prone to avoidance of conflict, the Japanese to its acceptance. But Japanese cultural preferences disvalue conflict. How can this contradiction be reconciled?

The answer appears clearly in the differences apparent in how the two cultures express aggression. For the Americans, the modal answer to the situation, "When someone insults him" is "he fights" (23.8 percent of the total). None of the Japanese give such answers and the difference is significant at the .003 level. But 16.7 percent of the Japanese answer "he seeks to get revenge"; 2.4 percent of the Americans respond in such a way. This difference is significant at the .064 level.

Where emotions are deep and the scope for their open expression is narrow, the channels this culture shapes them into are tortuous and the currents intense: insult, grudge, betrayal, and revenge. These are the classic themes of a society where imperfect communication feeds suspicion and suspicion feeds uncertainty and anger. In

Table 5.4. When Someone Insults Him . . .

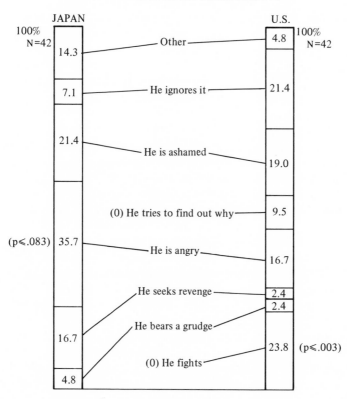

the greatest western expression of this view of the world—
where it is nightmare and paranoid—the protagonists are
separated by race and sex: Othello black, Desdemona
white. And an inexplicable element of arbitrary evil, Iago's
sourceless malevolence, is necessary to push the situation
to its outer limits.

The comparably beautiful Japanese statement of these
themes requires no racial or sexual gap to impede communication, no arbitrary ill will to drive the action onward.
Suspicion grows out of a social slight, betrayal out of an in-
jury to social status. In the great drama *Chushingura*,[4] insult and grudge, betrayal and revenge are not a social pa-
thology but the expression of social propriety. A more than
feudal honor is celebrated and depicted here and the outcome is not, as with the Moor of Venice, tragic misunderstanding and destruction, but an encomium to the mysteri-
ous workings of social harmony, whereby the human ills of
anger, betrayal, and revenge are transmuted into the pil-
lars of existential security and the preservation of an ultimately significant order.

Japanese, then, are not more averse to conflict in general
than Americans, only more averse to open conflict. The
proper response to provocation is not an immediate coun-
terattack but a careful and secret planning to get your own
back without violating the rules of propriety, which disvalue disharmony and disagreement. Conversely, although
open conflict is legitimate in American culture, aggression
and resentment are less often chosen there as response to
provocation than in the Japanese context. This is part of
the reason why conflict can remain legitimate. Where conflict is open, it is legitimate but avoided. Where conflict is
covert, it is illegitimate but accepted.

In the American political culture, conflict is relatively

4. Donald Keene's translation is *Chushingura: The Treasury of Loyal
Retainers* (New York: 1971).

legitimate, open, and rare. In the Japanese political culture, it is relatively illegitimate, covert, and common. The net of causation linking these propositions is complex but logical.

6: Identity and Responsibility

The data so far presented have touched on authority, power, hierarchy, equality, conflict, and harmony as facets of the political cultures of Japan and the United States. In this chapter the bedrock of human personality that underlies personal and cultural values will be the subject. We will look at what our informants want and what they think is important. These desires and values constitute a framework of personal identity and a set of personal responsibilities.

Table 6.1 shows completions of the incomplete sentence, "Most of all he wants to . . ." Americans are much more likely to say that what they want most to do is to travel, play, enjoy themselves, and have fun. At the same time they want much more to succeed. Japanese want to read, write, think, paint, and they want to do more interesting work or to improve their performance at work.

The congruence of these desires is striking. Both travel and play, reading and writing are uses of leisure. But the Japanese define their avocation as creative and active, the Americans as passive, enjoyment. Similarly, innovation or improvement at work and "success" are probably closely associated in practice. But the American wants the fruits of the process without the preliminary stages; the Japanese wants the process itself, the work and its improvement. He is not unaware that success will follow.

It is probably not unfair to say that the Japanese wants revealed here are more mature and realistic than the

Table 6.1. Most of All He Wants to . . .

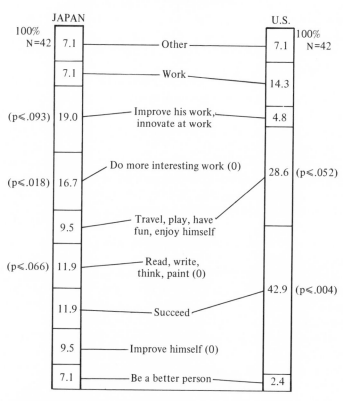

American. To want only to succeed and to enjoy is to want the prize without the effort. To want to innovate and to create is to want the thing in itself, the reality for which the prize is a recompense. The Japanese want to live, the Americans want to enjoy life. The Japanese want to do, the Americans to be done to.

Table 6.2 outlines responses to the incomplete sentence, "The most important thing in life is . . ." Statistically significant are the American responses, "love, family, personal relations," and "to be loved." The significant Japanese preference is "duty."

Because Japan is a family society where a firm structure of personal roles and obligations ties people to one another, "personal relations" can be taken for granted. Affection is gratifying but it is not "important." But the American lives in a society where personal relations are in flux and no relationship can be taken for granted. Love is more important because it is harder. Duty for the American, on the other hand, is a matter of contract. The fulfillment or nonfulfillment of contracts is routine. But duty for the Japanese represents not a contract but a total commitment. Just doing his job will require all he is. From it he will derive his identity. The American gets his identity from loving and being loved. These are his triumphs and his monuments. The Japanese derives an identity from honoring and serving.

The beliefs of these informants about what is ultimately important are perfectly in harmony with the classical moral precepts of their societies. They may change the content but the style is unchanged. In the western cultural tradition it may once have been that when one said "the most important thing in life is love" he meant the love of God or of one's neighbor. Now he is more likely to mean the establishment of a healthy heterosexual relationship on a mature level. Japanese samurai, too, three hundred years ago, saw duty as the underlying moral imperative

Table 6.2. The Most Important Thing in Life Is . . .

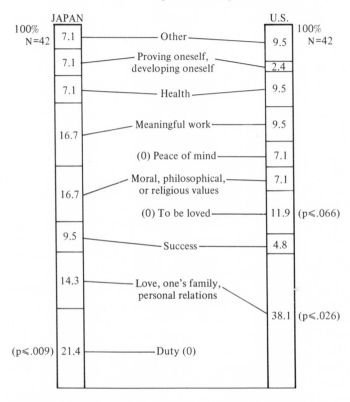

JAPAN		U.S.
100% N=42		100% N=42
7.1	Other	9.5
7.1	Proving oneself, developing oneself	2.4
7.1	Health	9.5
16.7	Meaningful work	9.5
	(0) Peace of mind	7.1
16.7	Moral, philosophical, or religious values	7.1
	(0) To be loved	11.9 (p≤.066)
9.5	Success	4.8
14.3	Love, one's family, personal relations	
		38.1 (p≤.026)
(p≤.009) 21.4	Duty (0)	

that anchored their lives in meaning. Duty was to one's lord. Does it change the meaning of this definition of responsibility if now it is duty to Mitsubishi Heavy Industries?

The Japanese group excels in the proportion that chooses submission to a concrete obligation as the most important thing in their lives. This is just as it should be; because a society like that of Japan, where social life is defined by an intricate interlacing network of harmonizing social roles, each with its own specifications for duty, loyalty, and obligation, needs to have instilled in the individuals who animate it a conception of particular duties and orders as the basis of their existence.

The Americans, on the other hand, far surpass the Japanese in their evaluation of the importance of love, people and family. "The most important thing in life is to be at home!" says one. For another, "the most important thing in life is the family." For two more, "the most important thing in life is to be loved."

This is odd. Japan is the "family society" of the sociologists,[1] and America is the mobile, fragmented, and pluralistic urban chaos of individuals where the family is supposed to be fast crumbling out of significant existence.[2] But it is the Americans who proclaim overwhelmingly—almost 50 percent of the total and more than three times as often, proportionately, as the Japanese—the ultimate importance of love, of the family, and of "being at home."

It is paradoxical but not illogical. Of course the Japanese can take the family for granted. At least this has been so in

1. Notably Kawashima Takeyoshi, in *Nihon No Shakai to Seikatsu Ishiki* (Tokyo: 1955) and *Ideorogii to shite no Kazoku Seido* (Tokyo: 1957).
2. E.g. Vance Oakley Packard, *A Nation of Strangers* (New York: 1972) and Philip Elliot Slater, *The Pursuit of Loneliness: American Culture at the Breaking Point* (Boston: 1970).

the past. Furthermore, emotional warmth is not drained out of the workplace in the name of the cold dictates of efficiency and rationalization. The Americans with their concern for being cool, for being unemotional, have created a world to live in where the only legitimate source of affection and warmth is *at home*. It is not surprising then that they long for the home and the family where the human kindness that they have denied themselves in the world of work and success is at last again available without shame.

It seems that the American contributors are much more likely to separate their work and their public ambitions from their pleasures than the Japanese. Work, for the Japanese, is the central part of life and it is fun, or at least much of the fun of life takes place in a work-related context. The drinks after leaving the office are taken with co-workers and clients. The women after the drinks are paid for by the expense account.[3]

The Americans we study here do not seem to have integrated their pleasures and their duties as well. They exclude pleasure from work more rigidly in order to "succeed" more radically and more rapidly. And this in turn may explain why the American, when he turns to "having fun," finds his pleasures on occasion violent, desperate, or clumsy. The search for having fun, being carefree, and "enjoying life," like that for security, is inflamed and enhanced by the singleminded pursuit of a "success" that forces all other concerns to be subordinated, at least on the surface. The American, it would seem to the Japanese, has given up a large part of life's satisfactions to pay for his pursuit of self-justification through success. While the Japanese lives in an organic and integral world, where life, work, and fun are bound up together, the American has separated work and play, success and happiness. This is

3. Among other accounts, David Plath, *The After Hours: Modern Japan and the Search for Enjoyment* (Berkeley: 1964).

the source of the poignancy of American responses such as
these: "He wishes he were young again." "He wishes he
were home."

Both groups are concerned with proving themselves.
They want to be adequate and able. For Americans, this
means something like "finding oneself," "finding one's
own way," "self-realization," "self-respect." This is a bur-
den the Japanese do not have to bear. One's "way" is
given in Japanese society, one's "self" is "realized" in
conforming to the demands of one's role, and "self-
respect" is not perhaps as important in an ultimate sense
as is the respect of others. The words of Polonius are not a
cliché in Japan but a heresy.

With the weight of all this to be sought, to be found, to
be realized, to be judged, by the *self alone,* is it any
wonder that the American of our study, compared to the
Japanese, is lonely and feels in need of love?

There is another type of personal sufficiency that Americans cite fairly often and Japanese never. That is the wish
to be *cool.* A banker, a Republican, wishes he were "less
emotional." Why should this be? For the American, ap-
parently emotion *in itself* can be sinful or shameful. Certainly showing it is. This is not so in Japan where emotions are legitimate as long as they are appropriate. For the
American, even the proper emotion must be stifled. He
wants to sanitize the social world, to drain it of all feeling.
It is possible that this is because feeling is a hindrance in
the climb toward the top of the social pyramid which is an
imperative for many of these Americans, but an imperative
to which the Japanese, with a role already given, are less
subject.

The Americans love the idea of coolness as they love
that of cleanliness. Dissociate yourself from the world. Do
not let it get to you. These are the strategies of survival in
an ultracompetitive environment. The emotional world is

to be handled with kid gloves, ignored if it begins to inter-
fere with important things. It must be *chilled*. Drinks must
be iced, dwellings air-conditioned. If the Japanese as a
traveler through this world is like one who sways gently in
the warm overcrowded murmuring pressure of a Tokyo
subway, the American is a lonely racer in a highspeed air-
conditioned automobile. He is going faster, he will "get
there" sooner, but he will not feel as much on the way, except, perhaps, his isolation.

The American seeks desperately for success. He is
equally and incongruously driven by the need to have fun,
to be happy, to be loved. He needs to succeed, and his
code keeps emotion out of his working life, which is seen
as a preparation for success. The more he strives for success and achievement, the more "fun" and "love" recede
into the mists before him. He is an unwilling Puritan,
staggering under the weight of an ethic his parents and his
teachers imprinted on his soul. But they forgot to tell him
why it was so important to succeed.

The New England countryside from which so many of
the American contributors come is distinguished by the
profusion of its chaste and severe steeples, the serene and
flawless lines of its white temples to a hard and demand-
ing god. Who has not seen them elegant and silent on their
green well-tended lawns? But the spirit has gone out of
them. On the sabbath the congregation huddles in a corner
of the spacious eighteenth century arched interiors and the
words of the sermon echo hollow around the pale domes
and bright windows of the church.

These men, the American elite, preserve in their souls
the vivid and uncompromising memory of an ethic of
struggle and accomplishment. That ethic, like the
churches in which it was taught two and three centuries
ago, still stands strong, clean, and compelling before their
eyes. But, like the churches, this moral imperative has lost

its living heart. True worshippers and true meaning vanish out of both. The American elite is driven by a command whose purpose and significance it has forgotten.

The Japanese elite is haunted by no such arduous and confusing motives. These men, responsible, conscientious, and dedicated, are wedded to their work not to prove something to themselves or to God but to prove something to their fellows. If the American is justified by the struggle to succeed and the search to be worthy of a love whose source is unclear to him, the Japanese is justified in the approval of his peers. This approval is given wholeheartedly and unstintingly to the man who is loyal to the duty he owes his position. Work for the Japanese is as central to life as any other single value; for the American it is important only as a tool in the struggle to be "fulfilled." Work is not a part of life to the Japanese. It is the essence of a man's self. For in no other form than in that of his daily work can his fidelity to the demands of society, to the demands of the particular conditions that define his role, be made visible. And if his loyalty is not made visible to the eyes of his fellow men, he cannot be justified and fulfilled.

Table 6.3 sums together the responses of our informants to two incomplete sentences: "His greatest wish . . ." and "He wishes he were. . . ." Among Japanese and Americans the deepest desires are these: (1) success, rank, wealth, and status; (2) to be a better person, to serve, to contribute; (3) to be secure, content, and at peace; (4) to be stronger, more able; (5) to be liked, loved, trusted, and respected. At this bedrock level of human meaning and value there seems to be no difference that can be attributed to cultural tradition, given the crudeness of our tests. And there is no significant difference between the Japanese and American samples whatsoever.

Table 6.3. His Greatest Wish . . . and He Wishes He Were . . .

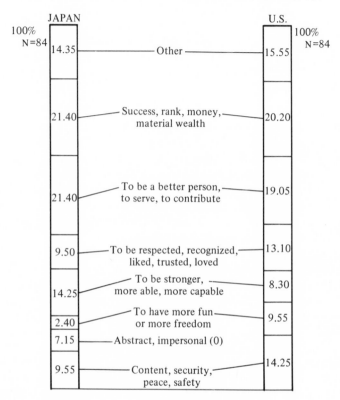

7: The Persistence of Tradition

In Japanese and American patterns of behavior there is a symmetry with cultural values and prescriptions that makes sense at a level beyond that of the formal analysis of structure and function. Institutions and social forms survive not only because they perform objective material tasks and satisfy material needs but also because they satisfy the subjective needs and maximize the values of the people who collectively make them up.[1]

This chapter outlines some of the ways in which the cultural values—beliefs—examined earlier combine to bring about typical patterns of politics—behaviors—for Japanese and Americans. We look first at some basic power-related processes: attaining power (advancement), manipulating power (administration), and enforcing power (decision). We then survey some of the elements related to political identity and interaction: private relations, belonging to groups, and the relations of nations.

What we are concerned with here is the political culture of the elites of the two nations. It is not necessarily al-

---

1. Chester Barnard put it: "The efficiency of a cooperative system is its capacity to maintain itself by the individual satisfactions it affords. This may be called its capacity of equilibrium, the balancing of burdens by satisfactions which results in continuance" (*The Functions of the Executive* [Cambridge, Mass.: 1964], pp. 56–57). The business firm of which Barnard writes is a special case of a more general phenomenon. It is not necessary to postulate equilibrium to recognize the mutually causative relations of institutionalized behaviors and culturally value-determined "satisfactions."

together similar to the political culture of the nonelite. But elite political culture is primarily important because it is elites, by definition, which provide the political activists who shape political life. The political-cultural rules of the Japanese and American elites differ radically, and these differences are pragmatically important.

Finally we are concerned with the views Japanese and Americans have of each other and themselves. These views are profoundly determined by political culture. This area of international communications is a vast realm still largely unexplored; this chapter points out only briefly some of the ways in which the meeting of political cultures may be favorable or unfavorable, synergistic or disastrous.

Belief and Behavior: Advancement

A political culture like the Japanese that prizes harmony and discourages and denigrates conflict will develop mechanisms for the selection of its leadership which involve as little open conflict as possible.

Many nonconflictual means of conferring authority are conceivable. One of the simplest is making it hereditary. This device will at least limit conflict to that among siblings. When, during the Heian period, the Chinese system of rule by examination-selected bureaucrats was introduced into Japan, it was quickly felt to be unsuitable. Examinations were discarded in favor of inheritance as a means of naming the scholar-officials.[2] This practice still lives on in all societies in which being born into an exalted family improves a child's chances of "inheriting" exalted position. Inasmuch as this seems right and fitting to the populace at large because of cultural imperatives limiting conflict and promoting social harmony and order, it

2. George Sansom, *A History of Japan to 1334* (Stanford: 1958), pp. 108–116.

becomes an organic social bond; in the absence of these cultural values, it appears an injustice. One way to measure the persistence of this particular cultural tradition would be to examine the extent of, and the rate of change in, social mobility.[3]

Another nonconflictual means of choosing leaders is by rotation. This is a practice generally adopted where the burdens of office are heavy and the rewards are light. So professors at a university will each serve their term as chairman of the department, after three years gladly relinquishing to their successors the problems of people and politics for the pleasures of books.

The rotation system too has been practiced in Japan, most notably in the bureaucracy of the Tokugawa period. Here the custom known as *tsukiban* limited the term of office to a month or two and a given post was rotated among a group of two or three people. Rotation was justified by contemporary political philosophers explicitly on the ground that it minimized the chances for destructive ambition, individual dominance, and dissenting competition.[4]

Rotation in office can be combined with the practice of choosing leaders by seniority, or the latter can stand alone. Here again a widely shared human practice is institutionalized in Japan. Promotion by seniority (*nenko joretsu*) has traditionally been the usual Japanese method of leadership selection. If individualism and open conflict in Japan are gaining increased legitimacy, then this technique can be expected to dwindle in importance.

3. James Abegglen and Mannari Hiroshi suggest that mobility is not great in "Kindai Nihon no Shidosha," *Amerikana* (May, 1961), pp. 1–24. And Karl F. Zahl's extremely valuable work, *Die Politische Elite Japans nach dem Zweiten Weltkrieg* (Wiesbaden: 1973), confirms the persistence of the authoritarian and hierarchical tradition.

4. See Conrad D. Totman, *Politics in the Tokugawa Bakufu 1600–1843* (Cambridge, Mass.: 1967); also J. R. McEwen, *The Political Writings of Ogyu Sorai* (Cambridge: 1962), p. 88; and John Whitney Hall, *Tanuma Okitsugu, 1719–1788: Forerunner of Modern Japan* (Cambridge, Mass.: 1955), p. 33.

It would not do to argue that Japanese political culture has not changed since the Heian period; but the devices of rotation, inheritance, and senority have been used in Japan for a very long time and in a wide variety of contexts to choose power holders.

Inheritance or pseudoinheritance (i.e. adoption) is used among Kabuki actors, flower-arrangement masters, and family businesses. Rotation is used for committee chairmanships and political leadership posts. Seniority is used throughout the society, from the boards of the big trusts and the factions of the parties to the semilegitimate organizations of the criminal world and the "water trades" (*mizu shobai*) of eros and entertainment. These devices all succeed in establishing a hierarchy of power while minimizing open competition to attain it.

In the American political culture, on the other hand, open conflict and competition are not shunned but welcomed so long as they are confined within the framework of "the rules." Furthermore, the Americans of our sample seem to prove themselves, to demonstrate their own worth, not by fitting as well as possible into a given role but by scrambling up as rapidly as may be through a succession of roles. Their final loyalty is not to the group of which they are a part but to themselves. And the emotional impact of the concept of "equality" for Americans means that most of the nonconflictual methods of assigning men to positions of leadership—all of which seem to employ rigid hierarchy to guarantee social harmony—are unacceptable. Fearing conflict less, desiring power and "success" more, and insistent of their right to an equal chance at or share of it, Americans seem to be happiest with a system of promotion by merit alone, merit demonstrated preferably by conformity to universalistic standards, "merit" pure and simple without regard to personality, morality, or traditional legitimacy. "No holds barred! A knockdown drag-out fight! Cutthroat competition! A battle royal! Dog

eat dog! Devil take the hindmost!" These phrases, and the
social style they allude to, seem obnoxious and inauspi-
cious to the Japanese, but they excite a cheerful antici-
pation in Americans. Their acceptance of this kind of con-
test for leadership is facilitated by the isolation of the
individual, the atomization of society, the depersonalization of personal relations, and the reliance on success as
the proof of one's ultimate worth. The relation of the
equally strongly held American value of "love" to this cultural complex is less clear.

In American political culture, conflict and aggression are
permissible but the emotional and sensual drives are stifled; in the Japanese, emotional sensitivity is cultivated
but the open display of aggression is frowned upon. The
jostling race up the ladder of "merit" suits the one society;
harmonious hierarchical order soothes the sensibilities of
the other.

Belief and Behavior: Administration

Although the Japanese structure of authority may look
firmly hierarchical, it is sometimes suggested that the direction and the motivation of policy may come much more
from the lower levels of this bureaucratic framework than
would be the case in the American counterpart.[5]

5. See Doi and Maruyama as cited in n. 11 of chapter 2. Also, for example, Nakane Chie, *Tate Shakai no Ningen Kankei: Tan'itsu Shakai no
Riron* [Human relation in the vertical society: the theory of the unitary
society] (Tokyo: 1967), p. 146: ". . . in the so-called 'ringi-sei' . . . the
conceptions of the people at the top are not imposed on those below, but
on the contrary the opinions of those below are submitted to the top and
adopted . . . If this system is fully adopted . . . the man at the top can be
a complete fool and no harm is done"; and Hosoya Chihiro, "Miscalcula-
tions in Deterrent Policy in Japanese-U.S. Relations 1938–1941," *Hitotsubashi Journal of Law and Politics*, vol. 6 (April, 1968), pp. 45–46: "[The
U.S. leaders] in predicting Japan's reactions thought chiefly in terms of
the reactions of the political leadership . . . They had an exceedingly inadequate understanding of the important role played by the middle
echelon military officers in the course of Japanese foreign policy de-

Historians of Japan point to the process by which formal authority through the centuries seemed to devolve or be delegated to an interminable succession of substitute power-holders: lieutenants, viceroys, regents, temporary military dictators. Accounts of both the authoritarian Tokugawa state and the hesitantly liberalizing governments of the Meiji period lay stress on the pattern of foolish superior and clever subordinate; the one a figurehead whose role is simply to embody a symbolic authority, the other a manipulator, an initiator, a maker of policies but not the taker of responsibility for them.

Analysts of the still imperfectly understood history of the Showa Restoration period of ideological supernationalism in the twentieth century are accustomed to stress in their accounts also the role of a middle-level officer class which is supposed to have taken decisions affecting the survival of the nation in the most immediate way without consulting, or being subject to any effective check from, their formal superiors. These superiors, for their part, are viewed by Maruyama as nothing more than "pathetic robots."

Students of business administration are accustomed to point out almost unanimously that the managing elites in the world of the private firm are not strong decisive men, captains of industry, but men who perform their function, not by deciding themselves but by creating a proper cli-

cision-making at this time. . . . [They] concluded that in the light of the disparity of strength . . . Japanese decision-makers . . . could not conceivably decide on war. In this regard they made the mistake of applying to the Japanese in unaltered form the western model of the decision-making process and the conception of rationalistic behavior." This theme is also found in William Brown, "Japanese Management: The Cultural Background" in *Culture and Management: Text and Readings in Comparative Management,* ed. Ross Weber (Homewood, Ill.: 1969), p. 436 (he quotes Yoshino Yotaro, "Soto Kara Mita Nihonteki Keiei," *Bessatsu Chuo Koron: Keiei Mondai* [1964], p. 8); and in Michael Yoshino, *Japan's Managerial System: Tradition and Innovation* (Cambridge, Mass.: 1969), p. 257.

mate for decision by others. In this view, postwar Japanese business leaders are distinguished from their overseas counterparts by the almost excessive liberality of their delegation of power. If the military leaders of the Pacific War period are "pathetic robots," the business leaders of the period following "may," for Nakane, "be complete fools and no harm is done."

It is possible that this could be so. It may be that Japanese leaders are typically selected only for their seniority and that their consequent lack of ability forces them to delegate real work to their subordinates. It may be that the personalistic bonds between superior and subordinate discussed in chapter 2 are strong enough not only to make the superior slightly more inclined to do a favor for one of his men who does not actually deserve it (as in the case of "the letter of recommendation") but also to compel him to abrogate his formal authority in the face of opposition from below. Such a conclusion would certainly point not to hierarchy but to pseudohierarchy.

But the extreme argument that Japanese leaders are "pathetic robots" or "complete fools" is disproven by acquaintance with the men who are the objects of these epithets. The true situation is more complex and more interesting.

Its flavor is suggested by a Thematic Apperception Test story told by a division chief in one of Tokyo's greatest economic empires:

> This is a picture of a division chief conferring with the group of section chiefs directly subordinate to him. They disagree. The section chiefs are uncompromising because they bear the responsibility of presenting the views of the people who work under them.
>
> The argument ends without any clear outcome. The division chief is about to leave. Now the section chiefs gather around the oldest in their number to exchange their whispered views.

The division chief is faced with a dilemma. Shall he hold fast to the views of top management and try to think of some way to get his subordinates to agree with him? Or shall he respect the sincere opinion of the section chiefs and alter official policy unofficially?

In either case this company will henceforth face real problems. . . .

The problem is that in a social and cultural environment that values harmony and rejects open conflict, that stresses the group's coherence more than the individual's contribution, and that sees proper conduct not in sticking to the rule but in embodying the role—a much more subtle and delicate prescription for action—the style and the technique of leadership must differ. But leadership is still leadership.

The brutal application of "one-man" authority will always incite conflict unless it is seen as legitimated by tradition or prescription. In the American managerial context, as we have seen, it is legitimated by prescription. In the Japanese case, however, where the rules for handling conflict and exercising coercive authority are less emphasized and elaborated and where the traditions of rule are embodied in a different image of the ideal leader, nakedly unilateral decision incites a strong mistrust. This does not mean that the leader does not make decisions, only that he must make them differently.

One of the prerequisites for the satisfactory exercise of the decision-making power in this culture is that no one's ultimate self-esteem—his commitment to his social role—may be injured.[6] Furthermore, dissension or difference of opinion must not appear in the open because the group's harmony might seem to be damaged. Together with the importance of the group goes the deepest fear of the indi-

6. Compare George De Vos, "Role Narcissism and the Etiology of Japanese Suicide" in *Socialization for Achievement: Essays on the Cultural Psychology of the Japanese* (Berkeley: 1973), pp. 438–85.

vidual member of it: exclusion. And so no one must
seem to be left out of the process of charting the direction
in which the group decides to move.

These cultural factors act together to bring about the development of techniques of administration that are found
in the American environment only in the sphere of international diplomacy; and due to the American insensitivity
to nuance, prestige, and the uniqueness of each particular
case, sometimes not even there.

The epitome of these techniques is *nemawashi,* "root-
trimming." Just as, before a tree or a shrub is transplanted,
the roots must be trimmed back to a convenient length
well before the actual move takes place, so the shock of
changing policy in organizations must be cushioned by a
long and careful period of preparation. Thus all the loose
ends are tied up neatly, the plant to be transplanted is
balled and bound securely, and the chances of successful
transition to a new soil and new growth are made as great
as possible.

What is wanted is to prepare the proper climate of opinion so that when a new policy is voiced openly it will receive not the shock of surprised ignorance and threatened
security but the favorable reception of those who have
come to see it as their own idea. Everyone who might be
concerned must be sounded in advance, without an actual
commitment being made either by suggestor or suggestee.
The dangers of disharmonious conflict, of injured role-
pride, of involuntary exclusion, are eliminated as much as
possible by making all preliminary consultation nonbind-
ing, extensive, long-lasting, and discreet.

Just as embassies may maintain informal contacts for
years at the level of the third secretary and the unofficial
emissary before prime ministers, plenipotentiaries, and
legislatures conclude their majestic and ceremonious public pacts, so in the policy-making and negotiation process
of the Japanese organization the same techniques of diplo-

matic courtesy guard against the same fear and danger—
the outbreak of open conflict.

Everything must be sounded out in advance at the junior level because of the danger of public conflict and
damage to group prestige if leaders confer and bargain
openly. This leads some observers to suppose that it is the
juniors themselves who are arranging the accommodation
of interest and policy. They are indeed, but only as accre-
dited emissaries who may be in trouble if they exceed
their powers. Because formal leaders appear in public to
make formal declarations of policy after long preliminary
talks in which almost everyone has been consulted, their
role is not that of rubber stamps or legitimators only. Because they direct and initiate and coordinate the process of
nemawashi, they remain in control, but that control is exercised by different techniques because the men who sub-
mit to it are different in their perceptions of what is legitimate.

This pattern of administration was formalized in the system known as *ringi*, formerly much in use in large hierarchical bureaucracies of all kinds. Here a policy document
is drafted for the first time at the lowest levels of command
by the subleader at the operating level. The document is
then considered separately by the officials of all the concerned departments of the organization, starting at the
lower levels and working up through to higher ones. As a
consequence, the policy proposal is supposed ideally not
to be seen by any individual until all his direct subordinates have seen it, nor is it ever the subject of a formal
conference of all officials concerned.

In the pure case, this means that when the *ringi* document comes to the top level of the organization, it has the
seals of approval of all the members of the hierarchy
below that apex. It would be very difficult to ignore such a
consensus of opinion and impossible to veto it except by a
studied and negligent inaction. This unique development

of bureaucratic procedure has been cited by those who argue that the Japanese leader is at the mercy of his subordinates. But it is not so. Tsuji, whose description of the system is the best in English, takes as evidence of the helplessness of the superior an anecdote told him by a friend:

> A higher civil servant . . . once told me that when he thought of a plan or policy he wanted to effect, he could only send it as a mere proposal or item for future reference to the appropriate low-ranking administrator.[7]

But the "low-ranking administrator" did not send such uninvited memos to his chief! And a "mere proposal or item for future reference" would have some considerable weight coming from the very top of the hierarchical group within which so much of the emotional life of the individual is concentrated.

The *ringi* system is now little used, but it once represented a delicate crystallization of human values, needs, and proprieties into a formal structure of behavior. What that structure reveals is not the restriction of the Japanese leader to a purely nominal and legitimating authority, but the flowering of his real authority in an environment where propriety, prestige, and a virtuoso sensitivity to the feelings and intentions of others dictate a strategy of conciliation, indirection, and persuasion rather than one of the arbitrary assertion of individual prerogative.

In American political culture, on the contrary, a leader is respected for open activism rather than for subtlety. Even the word "leader" has had to be imported into Japan and naturalized imperfectly as *rida*—or even more implausibly as *wan man rida*. At its Western extreme the concept illus-

7. Tsuji Kiyoaki, "Decision-making in the Japanese Government: A Study of Ringisei," in *Political Development in Modern Japan*, ed. Robert Ward (Princeton, N.J.: 1968), p. 463.

trates by contrast the virtues of the Japanese style, as it shades from "leader" to *"Duce"* or *"Führer."*

Deeply embedded in the iconography of leadership in the West is the culturally specific bias that led a man as acute as Freud to elevate his dream of the family into a mythos of beginnings to challenge the Garden of Eden: that of the "primal horde," ruled despotically by a father-chief:

> . . . many equals, who can identify themselves with one another, and a single person superior to them all—that is the situation that we find realized in groups which are capable of subsisting . . . man is . . . a horde animal, an individual creature in a horde led by a chief.[8]

This Freudian paradigm of the distribution of authority within organizations and groups is an ideal-type exaggeration of a tendency found in American and European political cultures, but strange to that of Japan. In the format of authority of our American contributors, power is formalized, centralized, and circumscribed. It belongs to one or it does not. There is no ambiguity. In the Japanese case, everyone has some right to be heard because of his membership; in the American case, there is no right without rank. That is why "what makes American leaders most angry" is to be crossed, to have their orders ignored, to hear back-talk. Deviations from the formal rules that govern the distribution of power in the American political culture are occasions for anger because any deviation from the rules threatens the fabric of social understanding. But the Japanese fabric is woven of more flexible stuff and its warp and woof are not adherence to the rules but sensitive mutual understanding of role-dictated exigencies.

This American formalization and centralization of au-

8. Sigmund Freud, *Group Psychology and the Analysis of the Ego*, trans. James Strachey (New York: 1960), p. 68.

thority is embedded deeply in popular mythology. The
sign on President Truman's desk that said "The buck stops
here" was in part an arrogant assertion of his ultimate personal right to rule. A more Japanese sign would have read
"We're all in this together." Lincoln is said to have concluded a cabinet meeting at which all his aides expressed
extreme negative disapproval of his proposals with the
words "The ayes have it." Admirable strength of character
for Americans, this is insane self-will and suicidal hyper-
individualism for Japanese. An American television com-
mercial shows a solemnly careworn tycoon pacing the
halls of a palace of finance or the sands of a very expensive
beach: "No one," intones a sympathetic and respectful
voice, "can take the ultimate weight of decision-making off
your shoulders." That is the image of the leader in American political culture. His final hope is in machines, not
men. The Japanese leader may use computers too, but he
relies on his men and expects assistance from them, where
the American is bound to a lonely affirmation of his personal responsibility and his personal prerogative.

Because the American leader is alone and because he attained his position by fighting for it in a more open and
formalized way than did his Japanese counterpart, he is
likely to be more active and his action will be greeted with
an optimism about power rather than a pessimistic expectation of the worst. Here is a cycle of cultural cause and ef-
fect: just as the continual flow of air and ocean currents in
their uniquely determined patterns shapes the climate of a
region, so the interplay of these patterns of attitude and expectation constructs, in the geography of society, an emotional weather for the local inhabitants.

The Japanese configuration is one in which the necessity of muffling open conflict means that leadership will be
more delicate and less arbitrary; because leadership is less
pushing and because dissension about issues has to be
disguised, open rules and safeguards governing the use of

power are not developed. And because there are not formal safeguards to prevent the abuse of power and because power acts invisibly rather than in the open, it is distrusted. Most Japanese expect a man in a position of authority not to behave well.

The currents flow differently in the American pattern. Conflict is open and is encouraged as long as it is carried on according to the rules. Roberts' Rules of Order—"according to Hoyle"—these are the canons invoked by the legalistic Americans. Because conflict can be open and because there are consequently strong formal safeguards against abuses, the American leader can be more active and more arrogant and at the same time he can maintain the trust of his followers. They, like he, have in the ideal case internalized the rules governing the responsibility that goes with the concentration of authority in one man.

A delicate and self-perpetuating balance of forces in each case creates a typical social climate. Intimacy, sensitivity, consideration, flexibility, caution, and mistrust mark the relations of leader and led in the Japanese organization; in the American, the distinguishing characteristics are conflict, depersonalization, adherence to law, disregard of the nuance, conspicuous activism, and confidence in authority.

Belief and Behavior: Decisions

After a leadership is selected and after a policy or a set of alternate policies is worked out, a final commitment to one course or another must be made by the process of *formalizing decision.* The techniques used to confirm choices as legitimate differ from culture to culture as differing political values shape different conceptions of justice and propriety.

In the Japanese case, the valuation of the group over the individual, of harmony over conflict, and of the particular nuance over the general principle combine to produce an institutionalized pattern of formalizing decisions that is seen in its purest form in the village meeting (*yoriai*).[9] The *yoriai* pattern represents the ideal image of how legitimate decisions are made and this image of harmonious consensus underlies the more complex and formal stylizations of making decisions in the modern Japanese world of big cities, big business, and big government, just as the heated debate and the formalized conflict of the New England town meeting may be discerned behind the decision-rituals of the American elite.

In *yoriai* decision-making, the subtle preliminary consultation of *nemawashi* is a prerequisite. Everyone must be consulted informally, everyone must be heard, but not in such a way that the hearing of different opinions develops into opposition. The leader and his assistants "harmonize opinion" (*iken chosei*) in advance, using go-betweens to avert the confrontation of opposing forces. After a consensus of opinion is reached by the iteration of compromise and minute adjustment behind the scenes, the *yoriai* meeting is held to allow the prearranged consensus policy to be suggested and for general public acceptance to be demonstrated. The ideal result is the "unopposed recommendation" (*suisen iginashi*) or the "unanimous voice" (*manjo itchi*). This legitimates decision: that everyone concerned agrees, that the group as a whole is behind it, that it is taken in such a way that process and outcome enshrine and embody social harmony.

Where these procedures are not scrupulously followed, the result can only be to deprive the decision of legitimacy and to perpetuate conflict. One Japanese bureaucrat writes of the first TAT picture:

9. See Nakane, "Traditional Patterns . . . in Japan," in *Leadership and Authority: A Symposium*, ed. Gehan Wijeyewardene (Singapore: 1968) and Steiner, "Popular Political Participation," in Ward, *Political Development*.

Some kind of conference, but one man is not admitted to it . . . this sort of thing will destroy the group.

Not to admit someone: that is to break the first rule of the legitimation of decision. But simple admittance is not enough:

In a conference . . . one man's opinion differs from that of the others. The situation gets complicated and begins to get out of hand.

Finally the heretic leaves his seat, but he can't decide whether to leave the room or not; he is still concerned with the outcome of the conference.

The other four can do nothing but go on with their meeting. They make a plan of action, but when implemented it meets passive sabotage. Their records are irrevocably stained.

This conference fails because the "root-trimming" has been inexcusably sloppy. Getting everyone together is useless without having prepared the ground for agreement beforehand and it is worse than useless to hope to make a decision and to legitimize it on the same occasion:

He presents a proposal at a meeting, but it is voted down. His feelings are crushed and he leaves the room. Behind his back he feels the others exchange glances.

When your opinion is crushed by weight of numbers, antagonism and enmity are born.

That extreme sensitivity, that tender concern for one's image in the eyes of others: for the relatively obtuse, insensitive, and singleminded Americans, it may seem almost paranoiac; for the Japanese, it is real and they ignore it at their peril. Of all the means *not* to arrive at a decision, the vote is the best. It guarantees that the minority will be publicly shamed, humiliated, ignored, excluded—all those things that, as appeared in chapter 4, "make one most angry." It is a prescription to destroy the group. An expression of this appears in a protocol to the TAT picture of the opposing groups:

> A threatening mood has settled over the meeting. The
> . . . anti-mainstream faction has been completely ignored by the mainstream faction in its high-handed conduct over the last few days. . . .
> At first they were dumbfounded that they could be so callously ignored. Now one can see on their faces an expression of hatred for the mainstream. . . . The anti-mainstream faction resorts to a mass walkout.

Because the group must be maintained, no decision is preferable to a decision reached at the cost of setting faction against faction, bringing conflict into the open, and sowing the seeds of enmity and revenge by excluding or humiliating the minority. The *yoriai* pattern of consensus arranged informally in advance maximizes the chances in this political culture that some decision will be reached and that, being arranged in accord with the deepest values of the participants, it will be binding and legitimate.

The American pattern of legitimacy is entirely different because it responds to different cultural values. For the Americans of our contributing group, it is the individual's "success," not the group's cohesion, that is ultimately important. For them, a man is judged in some sense by an abstract standard against which he stands alone to be measured, not by the opinions of others in the social matrix within which he finds his niche. For them, conflict is not a sign of group decay but of individual energy. Heated confrontation is not a chaos that signals the imminent breakup of the group, it is rather seen as the blows on the steel that will forge a decision. The implicit model is trial by combat. The motions, seconds, counter-motions, objections, caucuses, the parliamentary juggernaut of the majority, all reveal the medieval trust that God is on the side of the winner.

Not the group but the individual, not harmony but conflict, not the particular nuance of the uniquely delicate situation but the legalistic yardstick of the general and universal principle are the key values. Stubborn, insensitive, self-centered, absurdly confident that legitimacy arises out of the ritualization of conflict according to the rules, the Americans of our sample have developed a decision-legitimating model that works for them. But Japanese use it only at some cost in anger, outrage, and abrasion. And what tedium, what boredom, what clumsy straining after elusive nuance for the Americans to decide things Japanese style, when they want always to solve the problem by cutting the Gordian knot or by using the sword on their opponents.

The words we use, like crystals from a mine, may reveal an ore of true meaning compressed and accreted at the deepest levels of cultural history. For Japanese, to decide is *matomeru:* to gather, to collect, to bring together like a flock of birds in a tree. Legitimate decisions are the sum of the contributions of all.

But to the Americans, to decide is *de-cidere,* to cut off. "Decision," like "incision," smacks of the surgeon's knife. Debate is *cut off;* the vote *splits* the group into majority and minority. Decision for Americans is a narrowing down to one alternative among many. For the Japanese, it is the coalescence of the only possible compromise out of all.[10]

Belief and Behavior: Private Relations

Dealing with Americans is hard because of their stress on individual autonomy, their admiration for ritual conflict and their relative insensitivity and unpredictability in personal relations.

10. It does not do to push etymological argument too far. For Japanese also has *danjiru/kotowaru,* whose ideographic image is an axe in the teeth and which means to cut—to decide (in the negative, implied). And there is *ketsu/kimeru,* where the image of decision is that of a river flooding through broken dikes: an overwhelming confluence.

Because they see their own "fulfillment" as an absolute value, they often fail to extend the same respect to the fulfillment of others. They stand alone against the world, anchored in it by no permanent ties of place, kinship or loyalty. Each of them is engaged in a lonely race for a "success" he may be unable to define and which, when he achieves it, he may find himself unable to enjoy. This extraordinary cultural stress on the individual blinds them to the most obvious virtues of cooperation. An American television commentator at the 1972 Olympic games went into flights of panegyric rhapsody on the theme, "Each one must run the marathon alone!"—but he ignored the scene the camera was focused on shortly before: three runners pacing each other and blocking off individual challengers in their strategy of team effort.

Self-isolated in this way, they defend that isolation by what often appears to be a willful insensitivity to the nuances of personal contact. They reject or ignore an intimate relationship because it will stand in the way of getting the job done and they are clumsy in intimate relationships because of the habit of rejection. Do not feel hurt if an American you must deal with snubs you. His cutting you off personally is only a part of his perversely determined excision of all personal relationships from his public life. That he disciplines himself in this way to purify his life of the germs of emotional intimacy does not mean he does not want or need it. But because he wants true relationships so deeply, and against his will, he is clumsy, grudging, and frightened if he allows them to develop. If you were in Japan ten years ago, there were probably flowers in your bathroom and a pile of night soil beneath its floor. The American, in his hygienic distaste for the impurity of physical and emotional reality, can reject both excrement and flowers. He may equate them.

Because he lives in a world of atomized individuals, not in a community, he requires laws and rules to bind him to others, to make up for the lack of the cement of individual obligation and intimate respect. When the rules are violated, he is outraged: he cannot stand *unfairness*. Of course the unfairness he complains of is usually the sort that injures him. Unfairness to others can be easily excused as good tough competition—a slight excess of praiseworthy zeal in the glorious stick-bashing game of life.

The idea of human relationships as contracts is carried to an extreme in the current American idea of contract marriage. If there is a personal bond that remains deeply and intimately illogical, unorganized by the passion of rationality, a commitment that transcends "rules," the Americans will remedy it.

One must not expect emotional constancy or predictability from them, whose ritual rhetoric and whose deepest feelings sanctify change and individual development. Do not make the mistake of thinking of the American you deal with as a man with a role, to which he feels an obligation and by which he defines his duty. His duty is to that self he prizes so much and his obligation and honor is to be free—of roles, of commitments, and of ties. His life is continual conflict and struggle, but you will insult him if you regard him as a soldier, disciplined, obedient, a cog in a machine. Remember that his own deepest image of himself is "the lone ranger": tough, aggressive, capable, he fights for himself alone and rides on after each episode of his personal drama is done.[11]

Even his affection is expressed aggressively and his jocular insults are not an ignorant or willful disregard of the other's feelings but an oddly ritualized expression of masculine solidarity: they are "only kidding."

11. This was written before Henry Kissinger's famous self-characterization in his interview with Oriana Fallaci. Kissinger is here quite typically American. Fallaci, ed., "Kissinger: Interview," *New Republic,* 167 : 17–22 (December 16, 1972).

When he seems to disregard the obligations of solidarity, when he evades the demands of intimacy, when he slips out of his relationships to go on to a new "fulfillment"— when Lieutenant Pinkerton deserts Cio-cio-san—he does not mean to be irresponsible. As one American respondent wrote, "A truly close friend is one you don't have to correspond with."

Americans dealing with Japanese, conversely, will do well to remind themselves that they do not meet each other as individuals but as representatives of social roles and that the obligations of intercourse are not to abstract and general rules interpreted by contract but to the demands of a respect for the particular quality and shape of the parts oneself and the other are playing.

This means that frictions, insults, slights that the thicker-skinned Americans might disregard, are unforgivable blows to the esteem of the Japanese. He *is* his role. The American, his precious and abstract selfhood not involved, can take lightly the clash of goals, the abrasion of misunderstanding, the clumsiness of personal interaction that results when the world is seen as an arena of conflict where the public rules and the private rules are different. For the Japanese, private self equals public persona and there is only one set of rules for both.

If your Japanese counterpart is going to regard you as the representative of a role and not as an individual, it is very important to see that the role selected is one you want to play and that you know the script. Most non-Japanese find themselves involuntarily playing the role of the "outsider." This is highly satisfactory inasmuch as ignorance of civilized niceties is expected and much tolerant allowance is made for it. But there is no provision in this role for true exchange or more than formal communication. Find a good role or invent one. Teacher, student, buyer, seller, lender, borrower, master, servant, lover, beloved, protector, protégé—all these parts have scripts in the drama of Japanese life; but improvisation is not viewed with a great deal of favor. To forget your lines or to transpose a scene from Act 3 to Act 1 will infuriate the rest of the cast and will puzzle or disturb the audience. The satisfaction of this drama lies in its predictability; the unexpected is not only an aesthetic but a moral failure. "There is a time and a place for everything" is the quintessential wisdom of Japanese society. Woe to the one who gets time or place mixed up.

Because roles are inflexible, personal contact has to be flexible. Learn to express and to detect a wordless benevolence, and unspoken intimacy, an appreciation of nuance, an assurance of trust that cannot be spoken. Develop a sensitivity to emotional tones beyond the range of those you need to know for a cruder Western music. If a man is hurt or resentful, he will not tell you; it is your duty to know without being told. Feel much and speak little; to speak much and feel little will be your most characteristic mistake in Japanese eyes.

Be sensitive to nuance, adept at prearrangement, above all be unsurprising and *reliable*. These things shape that loyalty to others and to social demands that is the greatest Japanese virtue. Their absence proves your insincerity; a man who is not sincerely committed cannot be trusted; and a man who cannot be trusted has no part to play.

Belief and Behavior: Belonging to Groups

An important thing to remember about Americans in groups is that they give little true loyalty to them. Their sense of comradeship (*nakama-ishiki*) and their feelings of solidarity (*ittai-kan*) are relatively undeveloped. After the emotional bonds of adolescence—the fraternity, the football team, or the delinquent gang—they pass on to an adulthood in which true belonging is ritualized and playfully postured only at college reunions and at the conventions of those artificial collectivities—Elks, Shriners, Masons, the American Legion—which so pathetically mimic and attempt to substitute for the missing reality of the true group.

Their ultimate concern is with themselves: their individual achievement, their individual fulfillment, their individual salvation. That "you must run the marathon alone" is not strictly true, but they believe it.

As a consequence, their social groups and organizations have little coherence. They are not clearcut, but membership shifts and flows easily. They are not coherent and of one mind: quick decision does not mean quick implementation of decision.[12] It is also true, however, that these American groups, in which so little emotion is invested and in which so much open conflict and disorganization is apparent, can survive strains that might destroy a Japanese collectivity. Because they are not ultimately important, they can tolerate threats that others, where coherence is more essential, cannot. The biggest group of all, the abstraction called "America," survives violent political antagonisms and fierce conflicts of local and ethnic loyalties because it is *not* the most important thing in the world. More important than black power or white power is personal power and more important than allegiance to the flag and the republic for which it stands is allegiance to oneself.

Americans give little of themselves to groups. They form them for specific tasks and discard them when their usefulness is over. Their groups lack a true and inward autonomous life of their own. Paradoxically enough, this makes them flexible, strong, and toughly tolerant of conflict—as long as their usefulness is apparent.

If Americans find fulfillment alone, Japanese seem to find it often in "membership." The great French social scientist Durkheim hypothesized that at all times and places

12. This is a point first made by James C. Abegglen.

what men really worship is their own society. But in Japan, more than elsewhere, the small group can be God.[13]

This means a constant proliferation of circles (*kai*), cliques (*batsu*), bodies (*dan*), factions (*ha*), and "professional worlds" (*dan*). A man can be defined by his place in this system of interlocking memberships. Such groupings, formal and informal, big and little, centered around work and play, receive dedication from those who make them up and give identity in return. This phenomenon exists only as a pale shadow in the American social world. An ideal grouping is all enveloping, it leaves no need of its members unsatisfied. It is a haven of warmth, security, and identity, like a family—it wraps one in family feeling.[14]

As a consequence, the Japanese are virtuoso organizers and team members as long as there is a harmony of interests. Cooperation is flexible, swift and smooth. Large Japanese organizations are able to make a coordinated response to changing conditions that is quicker, quieter, and more calculated than that of their American counterparts. Mutual identification, imaginative planning, and insistence on consensus combine here to demonstrate the efficient virtues of an active social harmony at its best.

But the deification of the group can go too far. One danger is overidentification with one's own co-members, so that the division between insider and outsider becomes absolute. In such a case, overall social unity breaks down and in its place emerges a segmented series of isolated social subunits, each mistrustful of the others and unable to communicate or to cooperate effectively with them. This is the phenomenon Maruyama has named *takotsuboka*.[15] Another danger of extreme group consciousness

13. James Dator said this, in *Soka Gakkai, Builders of the Third Civilization: American and Japanese Members* (Seattle: 1965), p. 14.

14. This language is that of Maruyama and Nakane.

15. *Takotsuboka*, literally, the tendency toward an "octopus-pot" structure: a social pattern in which many similar groups coexist with no communication between them, like so many octopus-pots stacked by fishermen on the beach.

is the proliferation of informal subgroups. Where the formal group is too large or too cold to function as its members expect it to, smaller informal groups coalesce and reproduce at a rate that threatens the organic harmony of the larger body. This unbridled cancerous proliferation of mistrustful and mutually antagonistic informal groupings is the dark side of the idyllic Japanese dream of the splendid, organic, peaceful, harmonious society.

From the American point of view, such an emphasis on the group at the expense of the individual can have two unfortunate consequences. It blurs authority and intensifies the amount of manipulation, bargaining, and negotiation necessary to get things done quickly (of course that authority be clearcut is more important to Americans than to Japanese). And it may lead to a paralysis of decision. Where interests within the group are basically opposed, it is impossible to cut off debate or to decide by arbitrary and mechanical means. Thus, policy outcomes in this situation tend to be superficial, meaningless, offensive to no one (*atari-sawarino nai*) or nonexistent. The worst possibility in the Japanese system of decision-making is a council in which consensus is impossible. At a time that demands action, no action is taken: a fatal dysfunction of an otherwise functional process.

Working and living in the Japanese context, then, it is important not to become locked into a grouping whose social and emotional exclusivity bars communication and flexibility in the wider society. And in any social interaction it is essential that the self-identification of the participants be prevented from degenerating into "us" and "them." Across *that* gap real contact can become impossible. But this is true in all societies.

Relations of Nations

One of the most dangerous delusions of international relations, and one that is almost impossible to cure, is the

habit of mind that sees nations as people. If the government of England fails to support the government of France
when support is expected, no matter how technical or trivial the issue may be, John Bull has betrayed Marianne,
and for millions it is a mother or sister or daughter who has
been raped and jilted. America is always "the beautiful,"
Columbia with calm face and torch lifted—except when it
is the bloated and lecherous Uncle Sam, long arms extended to rake off illicit profits and to strip scanty garments
from other "mother"-lands. And Japan is "our country,"
wagakuni, the source of the sun, the land of the reed
plains, the central blessed portion of the world, under the
special care of the heaven-shining Sun Goddess.

Both Americans and Japanese, like most other tribes,
personalize their nations in this way and feel personally
hurt when their country is "injured." The incremental
gains and losses, the making and breaking of agreements
with limited and particular value, the complex processes
of arranging international coexistence, which ought to be
the province of men of business and diplomacy with no
shred of fantasy or delusion to cloud an essentially cold
and practical approach to mutual benefit—these processes
become for those who watch the news and read the papers, and, even worse, for the men who negotiate, a lurid
dream in which nations garbed as people rape, cheat,
starve, betray, and stab (usually in the back). Only oc-
casionally do these numinous and unreal figures shake
hands or go to bed together.

Americans, when they define themselves as a "nation"
as well as when they act as individuals, are extraordinarily
confident of their own righteousness. America is the
biggest and the best and, like the authoritative men in our
survey, what angers it most is "to be crossed." Acquies-
cence to American wishes is demanded of the rest of the
world as if by right. Cuba had no "right" to be communist;
the North Vietnamese had no "right" to resist the just
chastisement of our bombs.

Americans see the world, as they see their own society, as a competitive arena in which "success" is measured by increase in power and status. Unfortunately, although the conflict of American society is ritualized and defused by a set of commonly accepted rules of the game, the international arena has no rules to humanize and channel aggression. Fifty years ago the Americans appeared touchingly anxious to establish such rules for international conduct. But the temptations of power and the anxiety of that power's fading have led the makers of United States policy to the opposite extreme: they break treaties and defy legal principles with cynical abandon. Their depressing confidence that the world is a jungle ensures that it will rapidly become one. They preserve their air of moral superiority while destroying the unique foundation—that obsessive legalistic concern for the general principle—on which it used to rest.

They still, however, preserve their regard for law as it affects their own interests. Uncle Sam hates to be "cheated." Does the U.S.-Japanese balance of payments shift in the Japanese favor? It is due to unfair Japanese restrictions on American competition. Are these restrictions eased to the American lével? It is due to the under-valuation of the yen.

The American concern for law in international relations has been eviscerated by the equally American concern for success. So where the most useful admonition to give diplomats of a nation dealing with the United States might have been in the past "don't be 'unfair'" or "don't cheat," now it seems to be "don't be uppity." But it is true, now more than ever, that the greatest good a nation dealing with America can do for itself and for America too is to insist on the rule of law.

Just as the Americans transmute the values of general principle, achievement, and conflict onto the illusory world stage where personified nations pantomime the crude personal relations of dreams, so the Japanese bring to international diplomacy, to confuse themselves and others, a similar store of particular fears and demands.

The greatest of these fears is to be left out, to be isolated, to be ignored. Since the Meiji Restoration of the nineteenth century the Japanese have sought to find a secure role for their nation in an international cast of characters. First it was to be as an honorary imperialist, one among the number of western countries that were to bring the blessings of civilization and industry—our civilization, their industry—to the backward countries of Asia. But the English terminated the Anglo-Japanese alliance and the Americans barred Japanese immigration, serving notice that Japan was ostracized from the company of the elite. The tenuous and ill-considered dream of the league of fascist have-nots in the thirties foundered on noncooperation and the consequent military and diplomatic clumsiness that led to absolute isolation and disaster in 1945. Now the United States is once again pushing Japan out of the niche that seemed, if not challenging and adventurous, at least secure—the placid, comfortable, and profitable existence as an appendage to American policy in Asia. Wanting to be *in* most of all and fearing most of all to be *out*, the Japanese have had singular bad luck with these emotional drives when they are translated into terms of the relations among nations.

A country that wished to create and maintain a mutually beneficial coexistence with Japan would do well to agree on a set of roles and to live up to them. Not to change directions without warning; not to create uncertainty but to eliminate it as much as possible in military and economic affairs; not to *surprise!* Uncertainty can be avoided best not by setting out a rigid framework of contract but by providing institutions for the long-drawn-out and continuous process of mutual accommodation, compromise, and adjustment that is suitable among clients, partners, friends, and allies.

Surprise incites mistrust, mistrust the suspicion of being

left out; to be isolated is to be betrayed. Betrayal cannot be forgotten and longs for revenge. Both American and Japanese cultures are strongly nationalist. Their cultural idiosyncrasies make dealing with them at the national level perilous and delicate. In their mutual relations, the delicacy and the perils are multiplied.

Saints and Samurai

The American and Japanese contributors to this study appear to model their actions on a memory, only half-conscious maybe and only half-understood, of what since long ago their cultural traditions have commanded a man to try to be.

The Americans: insuperably self-righteous, passionately dedicated to achievement, concerned to the exclusion of all else with attaining a "fulfillment" which they never dare to be certain of possessing, cutting out ruthlessly the merely personal, the emotional, the human from their lives as dangerous distractions, and serenely confident that their private progress and private profit will transmute itself into public good: are these bankers, these lawyers, these public servants and private masters of the most opulent and glittering empire of the twentieth century, are they not enacting a role and living out a code that was dreamed by their sober, smoldering, God-fearing forebears three centuries ago?

They are the "saints" their ancestors tried to be. But where their fathers stood alone before God, they stand alone before the world. Their fathers were building the kingdom of God on earth; they have built an earthly kingdom that is "under God" only in the pious platitude late and pharisaically added to the pledge of allegiance. Their needs, their desires, their fears, all were bequeathed to them by generations long ago. Need, fear, desire—these still shape their action. But how different the fruit of action where the original goal is forgotten!

Their Japanese counterparts too grow up and live and work in a land vitalized by a numinous cultural tradition, a spring that still nourishes the heart's root though its source is slowly drying. Their ethic is group loyalty, hierarchical subordination redeemed by human intimacy, disciplined cooperation, a furious concern with the honor of their role. Their responsibility is not to the universal god or the singular self but to the social nexus and the particular lord. Their dogged virtue is in conformity to social demands and in the hard work that fosters social harmony.

They are samurai without swords, loyal retainers to an imaginary master, servants of a code that persists in a polity that has outgrown it. For their discipline to be worthy, for that ritual to live, they must find for their hierarchical loyalties a new master, for their concern with harmony a larger and more vital social bond.

If they could understand each others' virtues, these men could teach each other much in the realm of political culture and personal relations. A mutual widening of understanding might suggest a closer approach to selfhood without selfishness, or help to define an ethic of social responsibility without social tyranny. Authority, in whatever culture, is always corrupt and must always justify itself. An ethic of power which transcended the limitations of these two antithetical cultures might suggest solutions to the problem of reconciling universalist justice and particularist personal concern.

These Americans and Japanese are devotees of work and change, although for different reasons. Their work will change the world. They may change it in the directions indicated by jealous righteousness or narrow loyalty. But they might also learn the virtues that are the neglected side of the images of saint and samurai—charity for the one, service for the other. The half-remembered codes of

long past generations have brought them and their nations
to dangerous heights of power. The saint may smother in
his righteousness, the samurai's loyalty may blind him.
The persistence of tradition guarantees these dangers. But
tradition, if it is an engine of change, does not always pre-
scribe the direction of change. These political cultures,
though their fruits in behavior may be dangerous if their
precepts are narrowly understood, still rest at bottom, as
do all our particular and parochial structures of value, on
an image—though unclear and distorted—of the good.

Appendix A: Research Methods

The creation of the data for this study began with a series of about sixty interviews with government officials and private executives of large firms in Tokyo in 1969.

The interviews were only loosely structured. They centered on the problems of leadership and superior-subordinate relationships of authority in the administrative bureaucratic context. Typical questions were, for example, What characterizes a "good" leader? What are the qualities of a "good" subordinate? What ought to be the relationship of a superior to his men? What institutional forms are most effective in shaping policy? What forms are effective in implementing policy? Under what circumstances? What are the strong points of Japanese organizational style, and what the weak ones? Is there indeed a characteristically Japanese form of organizational style? If so, what aspects of this form are most difficult for non-Japanese to understand and implement?

The interviews lasted around an hour. The respondents were not by any means a random sample, but consisted of men who were (1) accessible by means of personal introduction (especially important in the Tokyo context); (2) interested in and aware of the body of theory on administration and management technique (not a hard criterion to satisfy, as almost all Japanese officials are intellectually curious and role-conscious); and (3) willing to give up some of their time to talk to an academic observer (this last quality too was graciously widespread).

The interviews provided a picture of normal Japanese organizational structure and practice which was a useful supplement to my own three years of participant observation in one of the Japan branches of a large international bank. They also elicited some of the themes of attitude and personality which were later to be picked up in the survey material.

The second phase of the research was the formulation of the survey instrument itself. This is the M. I. T. Managerial Attitudes Survey (*Massachusettsu Kōka Daigaku Keiei Ishiki ni kan suru Anketo*), English and Japanese versions of which appear in appendix B.

The survey instrument is divided in five parts. The first part consists of straightforward questions about the qualities of the good and bad superior, subordinate, and co-worker.

The second part consists of twenty statements, scaled from minus three to plus three, with which the respondent is asked to indicate the degree of his agreement (plus) or disagreement (minus). The first five items are essentially irrelevant, being included only to set the mood of an inquiry into modes of leadership and for practice with the form of response. The second five items constitute a translation of the Rosenberg "Faith in People" [1] scale. This scale measures the dimension of basic trust or mistrust, conceived to be essential to the functioning of organizations; since no organization can exist without some degree of mutual trust beyond a key threshold value.

Items eleven through twenty of the second section of the questionnaire are a Japanese version of the Rokeach Dogmatism Scale. [2] The Rokeach scale measures rigidity,

1. Morris Rosenberg, "Misanthropy and Political Ideology," *American Sociological Review* 21 (1956), pp. 690–95; and idem, *Occupations and Values* (Glencoe, Ill.: 1957).

2. Milton Rokeach, *The Open and Closed Mind: Investigations into the Nature of Belief Systems and Personality Systems* (New York: 1960).

dogmatism, and authoritarian or intolerant attitudes. It has the advantage over the earlier Adorno F-scale [3] of a markedly lower degree of cultural bias.[4]

Part 3 of the survey is a sentence completion test patterned after the one developed by Phillips for his research on Thai village attitudes.[5] The questions in this section deal with relationships to authority (one through seven), dependence (eight through thirteen), aggression (fourteen through sixteen), dreams and wishes (seventeen through twenty), peer relations (twenty-one through twenty-three), and anxiety (twenty-four through twenty-seven). The rationale behind the sentence completion method is spelled out by Phillips in his own discussion of its use.[6]

The fourth part of the survey is a set of five stories depicting hypothetical situations having to do with superior-subordinate and peer relations in the work place. To each story a number of possible solutions or courses of action are appended, of which the respondent is to choose one. This technique as well as the stories used was developed by Hanfmann and Getzels.[7]

The final section of the survey consists of a set of four TAT pictures which deal, in order, with peer relations, senior-junior relations, relationship to authority, and conflict. The pictures are adapted from those developed by Solomon for research with overseas Chinese.[8] Japanese

3. T. W. Adorno, et al., *The Authoritarian Personality* (New York: 1964).

4. For its use in England see Rokeach, *Open and Closed Mind*, and for its use in Italy see Gordon Di Renzo, *Personality, Power and Politics: A Social Psychological Analysis of the Italian Deputy and his Parliamentary System* (South Bend, Ind.: 1967).

5. Herbert P. Phillips, *Thai Peasant Personality: The Patterning of Interpersonal Behavior in the Village of Bang Chan* (Berkeley: 1965).

6. Ibid., pp. 123–42.

7. Eugenia Hanfmann and Jacob W. Getzels, "Interpersonal Attitudes of Former Soviet Citizens as Studied by a Semi-projective Method," *Psychological Monographs*, vol. 69, no. 4, whole number 389 (1955).

8. Richard Solomon, "Mao's Effort to Reintegrate the Chinese Polity: Problems of Authority and Conflict in Chinese Social Processes," in

dress and facial structure have been substituted for Chinese in the Japanese version, and American dress and facial structure in the American version, but every effort was made to alter nothing else in the series. Since different artists have different styles, however, it is possible that there are subliminal clues in some of the drawings which bias interpretation in a manner in which it is not biased in the corresponding picture for another cultural group. This is at least a possibility of which the researcher and the artists tried to be aware.

The survey was administered first to groups of Japanese business executives and government administrators who were attending training institutes, management schools, and economic discussion groups. Completion of the questionnaire took place during regular class time. One hour was allowed for the task. In two cases the survey was administered differently. Here the instrument was distributed to the group on one day with a brief description of its purpose and returned on the next day. The sources of bias in this procedure were numerous. There was no time limit; completion of the questionnaire was done alone rather than in groups; there was nothing to prevent consultation with others; and those who returned the questionnaires (about 50 percent of the total) might have differed in some significant respect from those who did not.

As it turned out, the pattern of response of these two groups revealed no significant difference on any item from that of the groups who completed the survey under more formal conditions. There was then no reason to exclude these respondents from the sample at large.

The total number of Japanese respondents to the survey was 197. It can be argued that it is difficult to generalize from a sample of this size to the bureaucratic and execu-

---

Chinese Communist Politics in Action, ed. A. Doak Barnett (Seattle: 1969), pp. 271–361.

tive elite population of Japan in general, and even less legitimate when the size of the sample is cut, as it was later, to 42. But this objection loses some of its force when the biases which affect the composition of the sample are considered. The sample is biased away from traditional modes of thought and behavior, since it consists of men who have advanced within formally rational, bureaucratic, and nontraditional organizations. The training of these men too was designed to inculcate a rational, universalistic, and task-oriented outlook. That the physical setting of the survey was the classroom, the administrator a Western researcher, and his provenance M. I. T.—these factors too reinforce the Western rationalistic bias.

The null hypothesis in the survey was that cultural differences do not affect Japanese and American ideas about authority. Patterns of response which run counter to the expectation here, that is, "Japanese" patterns, can be safely assumed then to be more, not less, characteristic of the larger group to which we are implicitly generalizing than of the small group which is our Japanese sample.

In the construction of the survey a number of problems of translation, coding, and scaling arose.

Problems of translation could not be avoided, even with the use of the standard technique of translation from language A to language B and back again with no loss of accuracy. They were of greater significance in the sentence completion test items of part 3 because of the fact that English grammar is more specific as to person and subject than Japanese. In projective questions then the English forces a certain specific kind of projection: "When *he* did this, *he* . . ." Japanese, however, leaves the subject of a sentence or the actor of a situation to be inferred. It may be said that this vagueness facilitates projection; but the most common inference in sentences where the subject is unexpressed is that the actor is "I"—and this may make projection impossible.

To deal with this problem the Japanese sentences were presented in a number of different ways. In one through three the subject is supplied: a subordinate. In four the subject is "a person," "people," or "one." In five it is "most people." In twelve, thirteen, seventeen, and eighteen an inferential "I" was left alone, and in twenty the "I" was made explicit.

This sort of shotgun procedure was less than desirable, but limitations of time and of resources prohibited the pretesting of different grammatical forms. The use of different forms seemed to guarantee that at least some of the questions would succeed in attaining true projective status. In fact no serious differences in the efficacy of the items appeared; but a more scrupulous care for standardization would have produced a more reliable tool for research.

The only really monumental error of translation appeared on sentence completion item four: "Placed in a position of power, he . . ." For the Japanese version we fixed upon "Kenryoku no za ni tsuku to . . ." Unfortunately this turned out to be the beginning of a well-known bit of folk wisdom, so it was infuriating but not surprising when 40 percent of the respondents contented themselves sensibly with completing it. Comparisons on this measure are made then with a notably lesser degree of confidence in the significance of the response differences between the two samples.

The results from the Rosenberg Faith in People Scale were not used because in its Japanese version it turned out not to be a Guttman scale. In the English-language version agreement with the statements represents an ascending order of trust, so that there is a high degree of probability that anyone who answers a given question "trustingly" has done the same for the one that preceded it. Part of the difficulty was that item ten, "human nature is fundamentally cooperative," is a mainstay of the formal Japanese value system. But American values make this item the least likely to elicit agreement of the five. That the Japanese version of the Rosenberg scale used in this research did not scale meant that its results, while they might be interesting for within-culture comparisons, would be useless for cross-cultural purposes.

The American sample was gathered in the spring of 1972, three years after the Japanese testing had taken place. There are two problems with regard to the comparability of the survey results. The first has to do with the time which elapsed between the test periods. The American and Japanese respondents were men of the same age when tested, but the Japanese respondents were tested at a time in the world's history two or three years earlier than the American. And those years were not trivial; they included considerable upheaval in both Japanese and American politics. Differences in Japanese and American response on any particular item lose some of their validity as cultural indicators if they can plausibly be ascribed to the fact that the Americans have experienced a bit of history which the Japanese have not.

The second problem with regard to Japanese-American comparability is less troublesome. All of the Americans, as opposed to about one-third of the Japanese, took the questionnaire home overnight and completed it for the next day. Since this procedure resulted in no noticeable difference within the Japanese group, it seemed reasonable that it should not significantly affect responses across groups. But this assumption cannot be certain.

American and Japanese response rates to the survey differed, probably largely due to the differing circumstances in which the questionnaire were distributed. The Japanese, who took the survey either in classrooms or, if overnight, at management training institutes, responded conscientiously. The Americans, who received the questionnaire at a Yale reunion, with its abundance of more interesting ways to spend their time, returned only

50 questionnaires out of 300. Thus another element of bias is introduced: the Americans who responded are likely to be less convivial and more paperwork oriented than their nonresponding peers.

After the matched sample of forty-two Japanese and forty-two Americans were selected, responses could be systematically compared. This process entailed three problem areas: coding, the comparison of means, and the problem of statistical inference from small numbers.

The coding problem consists in the fact that the categories of response used were developed ad hoc on the basis of the predominant pattern of the answers, without a theoretical basis for categorization having been worked out in advance. This reflects the exploratory rather than hypothesis-testing nature of the research. But the ad hoc nature of the coding categories did not preclude further categorization such as the personalistic/prescriptive/performance trichotomy. A further coding problem lies in the fact that all coding of responses was done by the author personally. If this had been a psychological study of the kind in which rich and ambiguous protocols had to be reduced to numerical values, it would have been essential to have several coders at work and to develop a measure of inter-coder reliability. But the coding of responses in the sentence completion test and the leadership qualities sections of the survey was a matter of putting simple verbal responses in logically definite categories, and so the desirability of coding by a disinterested group rather than by a concerned individual was lessened, although it was not eliminated. Here too can be adduced in explanation only paucity of time and resources.

With two matched samples of only forty-two each, the problems of statistical significance assume great importance. The use of the chi-square statistic means that the probabilities derived are always approximate; only with an infinite sample size will the probabilities be exact. The smaller the sample, the more approximate the probabilities, and the less certain one can be that a given difference between the two samples is not due to chance. In this regard we have only rules of thumb to guide us. A conservative rule states that for tables with more than a single degree of freedom, a minimum expected frequency of five per cell can be regarded as adequate, although when there is only a single degree of freedom a minimum expected frequency of ten is safer.[9] Most of the comparisons of the responses of the Japanese and Americans samples are made on the basis of a two-by-two contingency table in which answers are divided into two groups: the one under consideration and all others. This rationale gives us an expected frequency of twenty-one in each cell, which would satisfy the rule of thumb. Alternatively, we can consider that we have most commonly a two-by-seven contingency table with six degrees of freedom and an expected frequency of six per cell. This too would satisfy the rule.

Another statistical problem concerns the use of Student's t test for the comparison of sample means in the Rokeach Dogmatism data. The t test assumes that populations sampled are normal and that population variances have the same value for each. In this case neither assumption can be made with impunity. Both assumptions are, however, often violated in practice. With regard to normality of distribution, Hays argues that "so long as the sample size is even moderate for each group quite severe departures from normality seem to make little practical difference in the conclusions reached." [10] And the requirement for homogeneity of variance in the two samples can be obviated by ensuring that the samples are of equal size.[11]

In any case all statistical measures of significance are

9. William L. Hays, *Statistics for Psychologists* (New York: 1963), p. 597.

10. Ibid., p. 322.

11. Ibid.

only indicators of the probability that one is justified in betting that the findings mean something. Absolute confidence in the meaning of test results is something that can never be attained. The moderate size of the samples in this research means that we must take each individual finding with a grain of salt; but when a general pattern emerges from the whole set of data, we may have more confidence that our evidence means something solid.

In this particular case it will be well to reiterate once again a number of caveats that have been made earlier. To wit: the eighty-four men whose ideas and values are presented here are not a random sample and do not necessarily represent the political elites of Japan and America as a whole. The groups were picked to be as like each other as possible, but they are not exactly alike and some bias may enter in the selection process. Eighty-four is not a large number, and patterns of response that appear significantly different could be altered by the shift of only a few people from one category to another. The reader is cautioned that the evidence is imperfect and inadequate—in itself—to support vast generalizations or elaborate theories. But it is evidence nonetheless, and of that we cannot have too much.

All data are always in search of a theory. Approximate or inexact data are more promiscuous in terms of the variety of theories to which they can be accommodated, but approximate data are better than none at all, for theories need data too. The social sciences are not alone in this predicament, but they are compelled to be more conscious of it.

Appendix B: The Executive Consciousness Surveys

1. American
2. Japanese

1. American Executive Consciousness Survey

This survey is one part of a comparative international study which is designed to investigate the attitudes, expectations, and ways of thinking of executives and managers.

We would be grateful for your help in carrying out this research, which will advance our understanding of the elements making for good human relations and effective performance in organizations.

This survey is completely anonymous. Please answer all questions as fully and frankly as possible. We are grateful for your cooperation.

Part I

1. In your own experience, what are the most essential traits of a good
    superior? Please name the three that first occur to you.

    a.

    b.

    c.

2. In your own experience, what are the most essential traits of a good
    subordinate? Please name the three that first occur to you.

    a.

    b.

    c.

3. What are the most common mistakes a superior makes in dealing with his
    subordinates? Please name three.

    a.

    b.

    c.

4. What are the most common mistakes a subordinate makes in dealing with
    his superior? Please name three.

    a.

    b.

    c.

5. In your own experience, what sort of people are hardest to work with?
    Please indicate three undesirable traits of this sort of person.

    a.

    b.

    c.

Part II

Please indicate your opinion of the statements written below
in accordance with the following example.

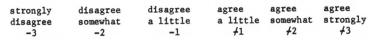

strongly disagree -3	disagree somewhat -2	disagree a little -1	agree a little +1	agree somewhat +2	agree strongly +3

Example: "The wisdom of age, like good wine, is best." If you
agree somewhat with this idea, circle +2. If you disagree strongly,
circle -3.

1. "Too many cooks spoil the broth".

    -3   -2   -1   +1   +2   +3

2. "Two heads are better than one."

    -3   -2   -1   +1   +2   +3

3. "The good leader delegates as much responsibility as possible
    to his subordinates".

    -3   -2   -1   +1   +2   +3

4. "The good leader inspires affection rather than awe."

    -3   -2   -1   +1   +2   +3

5. "The good leader grasps responsibility on his own."

    -3   -2   -1   +1   +2   +3

6. Some people say that most people can be trusted. Others say that
    you can't be too careful in your dealings with people. How do you
    feel about it?

Can't be trusted   Can be trusted

    -3   -2   -1   +1   +2   +3

7. Would you say that most people are more inclined to help others or to look out for themselves?

Help others   Look out for self

   -3   -2   -1   ≠1   ≠2   ≠3

8. "If you don't watch yourself people will take advantage of you."

Disagree   Agree

   -3   -2   -1   ≠1   ≠2   ≠3

9. "No one is going to care what happens to you when you get right down to it."

   -3   -2   -1   ≠1   ≠2   ≠3

10. "Human nature is fundamentally cooperative."

   -3   -2   -1   ≠1   ≠2   ≠3

11. "The worst crime a person can commit is to attack publicly the people who believe in the same thing he does."

   -3   -2   -1   ≠1   ≠2   ≠3

12. "It is often desirable to reserve judgment about what's going on until one has a chance to hear the opinions of those one respects."

   -3   -2   -1   ≠1   ≠2   ≠3

13. "Fundamentally, the world we live in is a pretty lonely place."

   -3   -2   -1   ≠1   ≠2   ≠3

14. "In the history of mankind there have probably been just a handful of really great thinkers."

   -3   -2   -1   ≠1   ≠2   ≠3

15. "In the long run the best way to live is to pick friends and associates whose tastes and beliefs are the same as one's own."

   -3   -2   -1   ≠1   ≠2   ≠3

16. "Most people just don't know what's good for them."

    -3   -2   -1   ⁄1   ⁄2   ⁄3

17. "Once I get wound up in a heated discussion I just can't stop."

    -3   -2   -1   ⁄1   ⁄2   ⁄3

18. "In this complicated world of ours the only way we can know
     what is going on is to rely upon leaders or experts who can
     be trusted."

    -3   -2   -1   ⁄1   ⁄2   ⁄3

19. "A person who thinks primarily of his own happiness is beneath
     contempt."

    -3   -2   -1   ⁄1   ⁄2   ⁄3

20. "While I don't like to admit this even to myself, I sometimes
     have the ambition to become a great man."

    -3   -2   -1   ⁄1   ⁄2   ⁄3

Part III

    Please complete the following sentences in the manner that seems most appropriate to you.

     For example: When they asked "What shall we have for lunch?"
I ... <u>answered, "how about a hamburger?"</u>

1. When his boss told him to do it he ...

2. When he is in the presence of his boss he ...

3. When his boss gave him an order he knew was wrong, he ...

4. When he was placed in a position of power he ...

5. When he was asked if he wanted to become boss he ...

6. The best way to treat a subordinate is ...

7. The worst way to treat a subordinate is ...

8. A really close friend is one who ...

9. When he found his best friend spoke against him he ...

10. When he say they didn't like him he ...

11. When he saw the others avoided him he ...

12. When he thinks of his mother he thinks of ...

13. When he thinks of his father he thinks of ...

14. He most often gets angry when ...

15. When someone annoys him he ...

16. When he was insulted he ...

17. He wishes he were ...

18. Most of all he wants to ...

19. The most important thing in life is ...

20. His greatest ambition is ...

21. What I like most about him is ...

22. It is sometimes good to hide your true feelings about a person
    because ...

23. In his relations with others, what he is most careful of is ...

24. He was most afraid of ...

25. His greatest problem was ...

26. If one is frightened, the best thing to do is ...

27. When he is worried, he usually ...

Part IV

The following stories depict a number of common work problems.
Please read each story and suggest the solution which seems best to
you.

1.   "The chief feels that the men under him are not doing a very satisfactory job. He asks his superior what he should do and the superior
tells him not to worry, things will take care of themselves. But still
day after day the output of the department goes down while other departments seem to work at full capacity." In this sort of situation which
of the following solutions would you pick?

> a.   Try to find out in a friendly and cooperative way
>   from the subordinates what the trouble is.
>
> b.   Intensify departmental discipline and crack down
>   on them hard.
>
> c.   Try to work through the most trusted people to
>   trace the problem to its source.
>
> d.   Pass the responsibility for corrective action up
>   to the superior.
>
> e.   Other (please explain).

2.   "One of the subordinates in the department is to leave the organization and requests the boss to write a letter of recommendation for him.
The department head feels he cannot honestly write a letter of recommendation for the man in question. Before he has decided what to do, the subordinate comes to him and asks what he is planning to do." In this
situation which of the following courses of action would you pick?

> a.   Refuse openly.

    b. Agree to write a letter, but, unknown to the sub-
        ordinate, write one giving a true and unfavorable
        opinion.

    c. Write a non-committal letter.

    d. Give in and write a standard letter of recommendation,
        notwithstanding his true opinion.

    e. Other (please explain).

3. "One of the men in the group gets the feeling that people are talking about him behind his back. When he enters a room people stop talking or change the subject. Finally, as he becomes unable to bear this any longer, he once more approaches a group of his fellows, and the conversation stops." If you had to face this sort of situation, which of the following courses of action would you pick?

    a. Ask openly what the problem is, and if it is your
        own fault, make amends.

    b. Approach one of the individuals in the group
        privately for advice.

    c. Examine your own conduct privately and try to
        correct whatever seems to be the problem.

    d. Continue to ignore the situation.

    e. Other (please explain).

4. "A new department head is appointed who makes consistently unreasonable demands on the members." What is the best course of action if you face this situation?

    a. Go in a body to the department head and inform him
        that this is not the way things are done here.

    b. Decide to resist the chief's demands by a program of
        covert non-compliance.

    c. Do the best one can under the circumstances.

d.   Complain over the boss's head.

e.   View the problem as an individual, not a group
     problem, and adopt a wait and see policy.

f.   Other (please explain).

5.   In the situation described above, all the members of the group

decide to organize a slowdown. In order for it to be successful,

everyone must join. One man, however, feels that the complaint is

not justified. His friends ask him to join them. What would you

answer them?

a.   Agree because of group loyalty and the ties of
     friendship.

b.   Agree because of the danger of ostracism.

c.   Resist the group because of loyalty to the superior.

d.   Resist the group because of your own conviction that
     the slow-down is unjustified and unwise.

e.   Other (please explain).

Part V

The pictures which follow depict fairly typical situations of human relations. Please examine each picture carefully and write a brief description of the situation below it. In your description be sure not to forget the following points.

1) Who are the people in the picture?

2) Where are they?

3) What are they thinking?

4) What are they doing?

5) What is likely to be the outcome of the situation?

Part I

1. I was born in the year _____.

2. I was born at _____.

3. My father's occupation was _____.

4. In my family there were _____ elder brother(s).

                           _____ younger brother(s).

                           _____ elder sister(s).

                           _____ younger sister(s).

5. I attended primary school at _____.

6. I attended junior high school at _____.

7. I attended high school at _____.

8. I graduated from _____University in the year _____.

9. My major was _____.

10. I am (single)   (married)

11. I am now employed at *_____.

12. I entered this job _____ years ago.

13. My present position is *_____.

14. In the last elections I voted for the _____Party.

* Answer these questions, if you like, only in general, i.e.,

  "I am now employed <u>at a large bank</u>"; or

  "My present position is 'Division Chief'."

2. Japanese Executive Consciousness Survey

マサチューセッツ工科大学
経営意識に関するアンケート

　この調査は経営者と管理者の(a)態度、(b)期待、(c)物の考え方を調査し、国際的に比較する研究計画の一部です。

　組織における人間関係と能率に寄与する諸要素の理解を進めるためにあなたのご協力とご助力をお願いします。

　このアンケートは匿名であり、その結果の利用および分析はマサチューセッツ工科大学の経営研究グループ内に限られます。

　質問に対してはできるだけ卒直に全部答えて下さるようお願いします。

　われわれの研究に対するご協力に感謝します。

第 一 部

1   あなたの体験から見て良い上役の条件は何ですか。思いつく
    ままに3つ上げて下さい。

    a.

    b.

    c.

2   あなたの体験から見て良い部下の条件は何ですか。思いつく
    ままに3つあげて下さい。

    a.

    b.

    c.

3   上役の部下に対する態度でもっとも好ましくないと日常感じ
    ておられることを3つあげて下さい。

    a.

    b.

    c.

4   部下の上役に対する態度でもっとも好ましくないと日常感じ
    ておられることを3つあげて下さい。

    a.

    b.

    c.

5   あなたの体験からみて、一緒に働きにくいと思われる人はど
    んな人ですか。そのような人の悪い点を3つ指摘して下さい。

    a.

    b.

    c.

第 二 部

　この下に書いてある文章について、あなたのご意見を下の例に
ならって示して下さい。

　「亀の甲より年の功」という考え方について、かなり賛成なら
ば（＋2）に○印を付けて下さい。全く反対ならば（－3）に○
印を付けて下さい。

例 －

　全く反対　　かなり反対　　やや反対　　やや賛成
　　－3　　　　　－2　　　　　－1　　　　　＋1

　かなり賛成　　全く賛成
　　＋2　　　　　＋3

1.　「船頭多くして舟山に上る。」
　　　　　－3　　－2　　－1　　＋1　　＋2　　＋3

2.　「三人寄れば文珠の知恵。」
　　　　　－3　　－2　　－1　　＋1　　＋2　　＋3

3.　「良いリーダーは部下にできるだけ仕事をまかせる。」
　　　　　－3　　－2　　－1　　＋1　　＋2　　＋3

4.　「良いリーダーは恐れられるより愛される。」
　　　　　－3　　－2　　－1　　＋1　　＋2　　＋3

5.　「良いリーダーは自らできるだけ責任をとる。」
　　　　　－3　　－2　　－1　　＋1　　＋2　　＋3

6.　人によっては「世間の大多数の人間は信用できる」といい、
　　又、人によっては「世間の大多数の人間は信用できない」とい
　　います。あなたのご意見はどちらですか。

　信用できない　　　　　　　　　　信用できる
　　－3　　－2　　－1　　＋1　　＋2　　＋3

7. 「大多数の人間は利己的で他人の事に無関心である」と思い
ますか。それとも「他人の助力を惜しまない」と思いますか。

助　力　　　　　　　　　　　　　　無関心

-3　　　-2　　　-1　　　$+1$　　　$+2$　　　$+3$

8. 「用心しなければ他人につけこまれる。」

反　対　　　　　　　　　　　　　　賛　成

-3　　　-2　　　-1　　　$+1$　　　$+2$　　　$+3$

9. 「つきつめて言えば、私のことを本当に心配してくれている
人は誰もいない。」

-3　　　-2　　　-1　　　$+1$　　　$+2$　　　$+3$

10. 「人間性は本質的には協調的である。」

-3　　　-2　　　-1　　　$+1$　　　$+2$　　　$+3$

11. 「最大の罪悪は、自分と同じ考えをもつ者を公然と非難する
ことである。」

-3　　　-2　　　-1　　　$+1$　　　$+2$　　　$+3$

12. 自分の尊敬する人の意見を聞くまで、事柄の判断を差し控え
る方がよい場合が多い。」

-3　　　-2　　　-1　　　$+1$　　　$+2$　　　$+3$

13. 「世の中は元々かなりさびしいところである。」

-3　　　-2　　　-1　　　$+1$　　　$+2$　　　$+3$

14. 「人類の歴史上、真に偉大な思想家はおそらく極めて少数で
あったろう。」

-3　　　-2　　　-1　　　$+1$　　　$+2$　　　$+3$

15 「長い目で見てもっともいい生き方は、趣味と信条とを同じくする友人や同僚を選ぶことである。」

    − 3   − 2   − 1   ＋ 1   ＋ 2   ＋ 3

16 「大多数の人は、何が自分のためになるかを知らない。」

    − 3   − 2   − 1   ＋ 1   ＋ 2   ＋ 3

17 「いったん熱のこもった議論にまきこまれるとなかなかやめられない。」

    − 3   − 2   − 1   ＋ 1   ＋ 2   ＋ 3

18 「この複雑な世の中では、指導者又は専門家に頼らなければ、何が起っているか知る方法はない。」

    − 3   − 2   − 1   ＋ 1   ＋ 2   ＋ 3

19 「自分の幸福だけを考える人は軽べつにもあたいしない。」

    − 3   − 2   − 1   ＋ 1   ＋ 2   ＋ 3

20 「こんなことを自分で認めるのはいやだが、時々偉大な人物になりたいと思うことがある。」

    − 3   − 2   − 1   ＋ 1   ＋ 2   ＋ 3

第 三 部

　あなたが適当と思う様に次の文を完成して下さい。

　例えば ― 「おひるは何がいいでしょうか」と問われたら、私
は…「おすし」と答えます。

1.　上役が部下にそれをするように命令すると、部下は…

2　上役がいるところでは、部下は…

3.　部下が正しくないと知っている命令を上役から受け取ったと
　　き、部下は…

4.　一度権力の座につくと、人は…

5.　「長（トップ）になりたいか」と問われたとき、多くの人は
　　…

6.　部下の最良の扱い方は…

7.　部下の最悪の扱い方は…

8 本当に親しい友達とは…

9 もっとも親しい友人が悪口をいったと分ったとき、多くの人
は…

10 嫌われていると分かると、多くの人は…

11 他の人が自分を避けていると分かると、人は…

12 母の事を思うと…

13 父の事を思うと…

14 人が一番怒るのは…

           …の場合である。

15 だれかに困らされると…

16 人ははずかしめられたとき…

17.

           になれたらいいんだが。

18   もっともやりたいことは…

19   人生で一番重要なのは…

20   私の最大の念願は…

21   彼の性格で一番すきなところは…

22   他人についての自分の本当の感情を隠すことは…

                        …の理由からときにはよいことである。
23   人間関係についてもっとも気をつける点は…

24   人がもっともおそれるのは…

25   現在の多くの人達の個人的な最大の関心事は…

26   自分が何かをおそれているとき、もっともいいやり方は…

27   困ったとき、人がふつうにすることは…

第 四 部

　以下の文は日常の仕事の上で起る幾つかの問題を述べています。
おのおのの文を読んで、あなたがもっとも良いと思う解決法をあ
げて下さい。

1.　「自分の部下が満足のいく仕事をしてくれていないと感じた
　　とき、上司に『どうすればよいか』と相談したとする。すると
　　彼は、『そんなことはほっておいても解決するから心配するな』
　　と答えた。しかし日が経つにつれて生産性が目に見えて低下し、
　　他の部門と比較するとその差は開く一方だと感ずるようになった」
　　このようなとき、あなたは次の中どのような行動を取りますか。

　　　a　部下と親しくひざをつき合わせて相談し、問題の原因を
　　　　見つけようと努力する。

　　　b　自分の部門の規律をさらに厳しくして部下にハッパを掛
　　　　ける。

　　　c　一番信頼できる部下を通じて問題の原因をつきとめよう
　　　　とする。

　　　d　上司に相談し、彼に責任をもって問題を解決して貰うよ
　　　　うに頼む。

　　　e　その他　（　）の中にお書き下さい。

　　　　（　　　　　　　　　　　　　　　　　　　　　）

2.　部下の1人が転職したから、紹介状を書いてくれとたのんで
　　きた。自分はその様な手紙を書く気にはなれなかったのだが、
　　部下はどうしてもと頼んだ。この様な場合にあなたは次のどの
　　様な行動を取りますか。

　　　a　きっぱりと断る。

　　　b　書くことを承諾はするが、部下があまり好ましくない人
　　　　　物であることを手紙の中に書く。

　　　c　職歴だけを手紙に書く。

　　　d　部下の押しに負けて、ありきたりの紹介状を書く。

　　　e　その他　（　　）の中にお書き下さい。

　　　　　（　　　　　　　　　　　　　　　　　　　　　　　）

3　　「自分は陰口をいわれていると感じたとする。彼が部屋に入
　　ると人々は会話をやめるか、あるいは話題を変える。ついに彼
　　は我慢できなくなって、同僚に詰め寄り、そこで話がやみ、座
　　が白けてしまった。」もしあなたが当人だったなら、次のどの
　　様な行動を取りますか。

　　　a　問題は何かとはっきり聞き、もしそれが自分のあやまち
　　　　　だと分かればあやまる。

　　　b　同僚の1人に個人的に相談し助言を求める。

　　　c　ひそかに自分の行動を反省し、問題と思われるものを自
　　　　　分で解決するようにする。

　　　d　事態を無視し続ける。

　　　e　その他　（　　）の中にお書き下さい。

　　　　　（　　　　　　　　　　　　　　　　　　　　　　　）

4　　「新しい課長が任命され、部下にいつも納得の行かない無理
　　な要求ばかりする。」もしあなたがこういう事態に直面したら、
　　次のどのような行動を取りますか。

　　　a　自ら課長のところに出かけて行って、彼のやり方がこの
　　　　　部門のやり方に合っていないとはっきり言う。

　　　b　課長の言うことは一応聞くが、みんなで意識的にサボる。

    c　その情況下でベストをつくす。

    d　課長の上司に頼む。

    e　課全体の問題ではなく、むしろ個々の課員の問題だと見なし、事態を静観する。

    f　その他　（　　）の中にお書き下さい。

    （　　　　　　　　　　　　　　　　　　　　　）

5　上記の事態で、ほとんどの課員が意識的にサボることに賛成したとする。しかしサボが効果的であるためには、全員がサボらなければならない。あなたがこのやり方に賛同できないのに同僚がしつこく勧めたらあなたはどうしますか。

    a　同僚に対する忠誠心と友情のゆえに参加する。

    b　同僚から爪はじきされることをおそれ参加する。

    c　課長への忠誠心のゆえに同僚に抵抗する。

    d　サボは適切さと賢明さを欠くという自分の信念から賛同しない。

    e　その他　（　　）の中にお書き下さい。

    （　　　　　　　　　　　　　　　　　　　　　）

第 五 部

　次の絵は日常よく見られる人間関係の状況を示しています。お
のおのの絵をよく見て、絵の下にその状況の簡単な説明を書いて
下さい。その際には次の諸点を必ず留意して下さい。

　1.　絵の中にいる人々はだれか。

　2.　彼らはどこにいるか。

　3.　彼らは何を考えているか。

　4.　彼らは何をしているか。

　5.　この状況はどの様な結果をもたらすだろうか。

Face Sheet

　　　　明治
1. 私は 大正　　　年に生まれました。
　　　　昭和

2. 私の出生地は　　　　　　　です。（ 都道府県名のみ ）

3. 父親の職業は　　　　　　　　です。

4. 兄弟は　兄　　　　人

　　　　　弟　　　　人

　　　　　姉　　　　人

　　　　　妹　　　　人

5. 出身小学校の都道府県の名前

6. 出身中学校の都道府県の名前

　　　　　新制　　　　　　　　高校　所在地の都道府県名
7. 高等学校
　　　　　旧制　　　　　　高校　　（　　　　　　）

8. 出身大学　　　　大学　　　学部　卒業年度（　　　　）

9. 専攻は　　　　　　　　　でした。

10. 私は結婚　（ しています ）　（ していません ）。

11. いまの勤務先は　　　　　　　です。（ 会社名又は機関名 ）

12. そこに入ったのは　　　年前です。

13. いまの職名（ 又は所属 ）は　　　　　　です。（ 例えば人事
　　課長とか販売部員とか課長とか ）

14. この前の選挙には　　　　　　党に投票しました。

Index

Yale Studies in Political Science